"With raw authenticity, Linda sh
choice of moving out of Hell on Eart
You'll be immersed in her bravery ana laser-focused spiritual integrity.
Use this book as a guiding light out of whatever hell
you're in. Linda has found a path that works, and
she leads us on it with brutal, loving honesty."

~ Martin Rutte
Co-Author, "Chicken Soup for the Soul® at Work: Stories of
Courage, Compassion and Creativity in the Workplace"
Founder, ProjectHeavenOnEarth.com

"Lost and in a lot of pain, I heard Linda speak of her recovery.
She spoke of the way she thought, the way her mind ran, and her
daily battle in her head. It was like somebody knew exactly what I
had been going through my entire life. That day I chose recovery of
mind, body, and spirit. What a true blessing it was to have her put
in my life at that exact moment when all else had failed."

~ Michael Cross
Recovering Addict, Pea Ridge, Arkansas

"Full of honesty and vulnerability, this book reads like a road map
guided by hope and resilience. Written from the author's experiences
dealing with alcohol and drug addiction, it blossoms into a book we
can all relate to on levels that are personal to us. We all experience
challenges in life, be it addiction to food, relationships, etc. This book
gives us a safe space to explore our past and be present in the moment to
understand the choices we can make for our future to help us thrive."

~ Diane Catrambone
National Board Certified Health & Wellness Coach

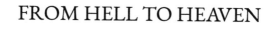

FROM HELL TO HEAVEN

FROM HELL TO HEAVEN

16 Lessons & Blessings to Inspire
Your Journey Beyond Recovery

Linda L. Fischer

The author was committed to write a book of integrity and quality. In that spirit, she is proud to offer this book to her readers; however, the story, experiences, and words are the author's alone. It is told from her point of view, which may not be that of the characters in the book. Resemblances to actual people and places may be coincidental. This book is in no way meant to offer psychological or medical advice. Individuals in need of psychological or medical advice should seek help from an appropriate professional.

*To all people walking a path
home to their essence:*

*On the path to self-discovery, know that
you are not alone and there is hope.*

And hope leads to faith...

"The only difference between heaven and hell is believing a thought."

~Byron Katie

Contents

Foreword

At this point in history, we live in a world where there's no one left who hasn't been touched by this problem... the problem of addiction. And I mean directly. Previously, I would've said indirectly or directly. But if it isn't clear to everyone by now, given the global pandemics and their associated fear, the unbelievable division in belief systems between people, and the way that natural disasters have created sudden changes in entire regions, this is a traumatic time in our society. And in the wake of trauma, everyone has to recover. We don't know how to deal with our trauma, so we turn to alcohol or drugs, or any of the countless other forms of addiction—marijuana, cigarettes, gambling, sex, codependency, porn, food, shopping, or perhaps spending far too much time every day on technology. So there's nobody left untouched. That's why this book is relevant now.

Linda, whom I know as Shekinah, brings to light the deeply human and psychological reality of the problem of addiction, as well as a deep understanding of recovery as a spiritual path. She unpacks this in great detail through the investigation of her childhood and life. This allows us to understand her psyche and soul, but more importantly gives us an opportunity to reflect on our own inner life.

The value of this book is that it serves as both a map and a compass. As a map, it lays out the pathway, following the first 43 years of Shekinah's life, beginning with an exploration of the psychology of a young girl and how she found herself in self-destructive behavior early on. The journey takes us all the way through to a mature woman, ready to embrace the unknown with self-awareness, presence, and courage.

At the end of each chapter we experience the compass—the guidance to navigate our life map. This comes in the form of the *Lessons & Blessings*, which are both didactic and inspirational. They offer profound reflections and insights for a deeper self-understanding and healing. These missives help us receive the most out of what we're learning and feeling. We benefit from the conversations she has with herself as a young girl. They also allow us to emotionally manage what we're taking in, because it's difficult, real, and rigorously honest.

The arc of Shekinah's life goes under the heading of the *Greatest Story Ever Told*. I would argue that everyone has one of those. But not everyone gets to express it. Not everyone gets to survive it and reflect upon it. Much less be able to turn the corner of their hero's journey and look back to say: This is what I learned, this is what became clear for me in the process, and despite the trauma, I wouldn't want it any other way. This is a rare and precious opportunity.

She, like me, relies on the wisdom of ancient sages to continue to guide her life. As Sri Ramakrishna said, "Approach illumination like a person whose hair is on fire would approach a pond." We're all pursuing our passions, but we most often do it in misguided ways. We do it in ways that don't ultimately lead where we think we want to go. Shekinah presents a real look at addiction, at being off track, and doing anything by any means necessary to fine one's place in this world and one's purpose beyond it. The last place she looks is the last place we all look, which is inside. It is only there that we have the real possibility of discovering what we came for.

This is a cautionary, hopeful, and inspirational tale. It's also a very strong invitation: Turn your gaze inward. If you heed the lessons of this book, you can avoid a lot of pain, difficulty, and misdirection on your life map. You'll learn to follow your inner compass and access your Destiny Path, which always leads to true fulfillment. And such is the power, promise, and possibility of this book.

The details of Shekinah's life are, of course, unique to her. Hopefully, though, you come to this with curiosity about how your own life may be reshaped through the reading of these pages. This human journey is universal. Always leave room for the idea that finding your way here was no accident. This is about our collective challenges and triumphs, and if you picked up this book, this is about you.

> With Love and Gratitude,
> Tommy Rosen,
> *Yoga Teacher & Recovery 2.0 Founder*

Preface

Before we begin, I want to acknowledge that I understand that we live in a culture where many of us read memoirs for entertainment. I invite you instead to read my story as a participant. Feel what you feel; think what you think; and notice the way your body, emotions, and mind respond as you take in the words on the pages. Be inside of yourself and see what's there.

This is a story of *our* time. *And* it's my time. When I initially set out to write my memoir, I felt the tension between revisiting my personal history and the desire to offer what I've learned from it. I found a deeper motivation—to share my life's experiences so others may know and feel that they aren't alone, and don't suffer in the isolation that I did as an alcoholic and drug addict. In many ways, this could be anyone's story of transformation.

This is also the story of opiate abuse and alcohol addiction in America. Pain from addiction is hitting crisis levels in not only the United States, but also across the globe. It's at the forefront of the political conversation, and you can't go a single day without reading another story of how addiction has affected another family's life. I'm sure we all know someone who has, or has had, a problem with alcohol or drugs. It's now a topic that's in almost every household, though it used to seem so removed from our daily lives.

The current time is also calling for us to share our vulnerabilities and secrets, and heal together. I was sitting in meditation 25 years ago (15 years after I began recovery) when I heard an inner voice say to write this book. This inner voice gave me the words: *Lessons & Blessings*. It has been both a beautiful and intense journey to prepare me emotionally and spiritually to write, and now share, this book. It is at once vulnerable and liberating to have the intimate details of my life on paper. My hope is that those affected by the disease of addiction, and their friends and family, find themselves relating to, and inspired by, these lessons and blessings, and able to heal their own life experiences.

Like all writers, in addition to my personal preparation to share this book, I realized I couldn't write every piece of my life onto these pages. I share a portion of the pain that shaped my journey, as well as the ongoing rewards that I continue to reap as I evolve. I decided to keep the beginning of each chapter as pure memoir—sharing essential turning points in first-person present-tense, as if we're living right in that moment together. Then, at the end of each chapter, I share both what I learned from that experience—the "lesson"—as well the essential nature of the experience, or what I call the "blessing."

I'm often asked, "If you could have a do-over, wouldn't you choose a different life?" And I say no. Both the pain and pleasure of each and every experience *are* blessings. I would do it all over again if I knew I would be here with you now. My entire life has brought me to this moment where you're reading these words and about to dive into the book. This moment is so precious to me. It's been such a painful, miraculous journey. Here we go...

Blessings on your journey,
Linda L. Fischer ("Shekinah")

Choice?

"May your choices reflect your hopes, not your fears."
~ Nelson Mandela

The room below looks cold, far away. It almost seems empty from up here. Except at the center. There, a knot of men and women in green hospital scrubs work intently over the body of a young woman.

She looks like she's in her late teens and not even 100 pounds, with light brown hair stuck in clumps to her slack face. Dark needle tracks mark the white insides of her elbows like half-erased pencil scratches. Her left wrist—wow, what a mess. A suicide attempt.

Who is she?

From above, I sense something—a Presence? I turn to face it.

Instead of a person, I meet a cluster of yellowish-white light stretching out in an endless line. The moment I see it, that light sweeps through me like an ocean tide. In this wave, I find myself floating in the most pure, unconditional love I've ever experienced. The love engulfs me so that I'm not even aware of myself as a person anymore. I'm lost in that love. I never want to leave the feeling of its embrace.

Suddenly I hear the words: "If you want to go back, you can. And if you do, your life will get better from this day forward."

If I want to go back…? With this offer now on the table, I suddenly realize that the body below is me. Or rather, I've been living in that body for 19 years. And yes, I *do* want to leave it behind. As Linda Sibert, I've been struggling with the terrible weight of life on Earth for a long time. *Why am I here, anyway? What's it all about? Could it really only be to experience all this suffering and insanity that constantly boil inside me?*

From up here—the girl down there… me—looks so peaceful. Despite the flurry of activity around my body, I have no cares. I can't remember the last time I've felt peace. Why would I interrupt this newfound tranquility by going back to the chaos I had just escaped?

But this idea that my life would get better, something about it tugs at me. Maybe more is waiting for me down there, things I still need to do. What could life on Earth be like without so much emotional pain?

Then, like a child pulling a kite from the sky, these thoughts carry me from the current of love where I'm floating back toward the body of the girl below. The journey that ended with me on an operating table in the hospital had begun a few hours earlier...

It's September 11, 1973, and I'm sitting in my parents' living room, something like the twentieth one we've had in the past 19 years. My friend Teresa and I had been dropped off by our friend Moe. Outside, a sprawling green lawn, manicured to perfection, is visible through the picture window opening from inside a room edged in couches, end tables, and stacks of magazines so tidy that the place could belong on the cover of Better Homes & Gardens®. All those neat and shiny surfaces give the impression that life in our suburban brick ranch is nothing but order and care. But in the midst of all that so-called perfection is me: damaged goods.

Sun streams through the large front window, draping itself over me incongruously—a pleasure I haven't earned the right to enjoy. The light holds my wrecked body as I fight a war with depression in my mind. Sitting in that living room, waiting for my parents to come home feels like sitting in hell.

How is this happening again? Haven't I disappointed my

parents enough already? Why can't I stay clean?

Facing my parents? I can't bear the thought. Somehow I need to get away from this deep shame and regret.

"I need some fresh air," I tell Teresa, and leave her napping in the living room. Warm, Indian summer air and sunlight slide over my face and arms as I step onto our front porch. I feel like a zombie as I walk to the next-door neighbor's house and ask if they have a spare double-edged razor blade. Without hesitation, our neighbor gives me one as I explain its use for shaving my legs. Back at home, I go into the bathroom and lock the door behind me.

I'd heard somewhere—or maybe I'd read—that this will hurt less if I put my wrists under cold running water while I make the cuts. So I turn on the faucet and slice, slice, slice, deep into my left wrist under the water, the thin skin breaking open like an angry mouth. From somewhere far away, I watch as blood funnels into the white basin and down the drain. I begin to lose feeling from the loss of blood and a relief washes over me. Finally...

By the time my girlfriend breaks through the locked bathroom door, I'm unconscious. The next time I become conscious, I'm listening to a siren's wail. A paramedic shuffles tubes and syringes, working feverishly to keep me alive. Disappointed to find he might be succeeding, I black out again, weak and disoriented.

The ambulance carries me to Scott Air Force Base, the military hospital that serves our area. That's where I find myself hovering above the body of the girl on the operating table, the girl who's me. In the end, I decide that she'll continue to be me, at least for a little while longer.

But when I finally wake up in the hospital bed, I wish I was dead instead. The doctors tell me I have pneumonia in both lungs as I struggle to breathe. I'm burning up with a fever and I'm uncontrollably urinating and defecating all over the bed. If my life before had been an emotional hell, this was a physical one.

Worse even than the pain in my body, though, is looking into the anguish that lines my parents' faces. I'm only 19, but I've spent the last seven years of my life in and out of psychiatrists' offices, psych wards, and hospitals. I've survived multiple overdoses, and my parents have lived for years with short and long periods of not knowing where to find me or even if I'm still alive. Now, after a month of staying clean, I've let them, and me, down again. And I've racked up another failed suicide attempt in the process.

But how had it even happened?

Four days prior, I'd begged my mom to take me to a local bar to celebrate my friend's upcoming wedding. At the door of our home, she pleaded with me not to use again, and I'd promised I wouldn't. It wasn't a lie, either. Of course I wasn't going to use. I had no intention of using, not then, not ever. I just wanted to get out of the house. I was starting to feel a little stir-crazy, stuck home alone with a head buzzing from too many difficult thoughts.

So Mom agreed to drive me to the bar. What a relief to be

laughing with friends again. An acquaintance asked me if I wanted to come outside to smoke a joint with him. Even though I was uninterested in marijuana, I said "Sure, why not?" After all, it's just pot, not hard drugs.

But the next thing I remember was waking up four days later at that man's house, track marks up and down my arms and the world around me a blur. I had just had so many hits of liquid barbiturates that I couldn't even see properly[1]. Just moments before, I had stepped out to simply take a toke off a joint. How did I get here?

My boyfriend Moe and my girlfriend Teresa, who didn't use drugs, had come to collect me when they found out where I was. They took care of me until they thought I was in good enough condition to return home. Then Moe dropped Teresa and me at my parents' house.

That's when I had obtained the double-edged razor blade and locked myself in the bathroom to kill myself. The thoughts running through my mind were that I was tired, so tired of being the person who hurts the people close to me. Tired of living with a family that felt like it was falling apart. Tired of feeling like I was the one to blame for it all.

My parents had tried to help, but they had no idea what was wrong with me or what to do. Following the advice of professionals, they had taken me to psychiatrists who couldn't seem to help me, either. At one point, after yet another move, I recall looking into the windows of cars as they passed me on my new walk home from school. Could one of these people help me? Could anyone in

[1] See Appendix A

one of these houses help me?! But no, they couldn't. I was alone. Completely alone.

I felt desperate to free myself from the emotional pain that was plaguing not only me, but everyone I loved. I hated myself because I was sure that I was the cause of everyone's problems. Selfishly, I wanted a way out of my own suffering, *and* I wanted a way to make their lives easier too. The razor blade was my best attempt at cutting myself, and them, free.

Because my dad is military, after the operating room, I wake up in a fog to discover that the ambulance that had responded to my friend Teresa's frantic call had carried me to a standard military hospital with no private rooms. One of my three other roommates turns out to be an acquaintance of my mother—a woman I had never met. She acts so kind toward me, this seeming stranger. How can she be so nice to someone like me? How can anyone be kind to someone who is such a failure, someone who hurts other people so much? I want to say to her, *"Don't you know who and what I am?!"*

My mind flashes for a moment to the tunnel of light, the *Presence*, the feeling of being engulfed in love. How I had longed to let it sweep me forever into its embrace. I recall the voice, telling me life will get better if I decide to go back. It had been a flicker of hope after so many years without it. But had I only imagined this encounter? Is there really any hope for me?

As the daughter of a military man, I know by now that I should live up to lofty values like courage, responsibility, honesty, justice, and loyalty. At church and in Catholic school throughout my life, nuns had also drilled into me the Ten Commandments and the mortal sins. On top of all that, my parents, who hadn't been raised Catholic but had converted by choice, worked extra hard to instill in my older brother Ron and me a heavy dose of guilt to keep us in line. In all of this, I have felt an intense pressure to be good, to do things right by these standards. I want desperately to please my parents and teachers and follow the path set before me.

But somehow I can't. And I haven't been able to for many years. To me, life feels less like a path to walk but rather a forceful current I'm swimming against to survive. I had been working so hard to keep my head above water in spite of the heavy stones of guilt and shame that fill my pockets. But no matter how hard I tried, I never measured up to these standards. The gap, this painful gap between what my behavior actually is and what I think it should be, plagues me constantly. Lying in that bed, I realize I have been judging and hating myself for as long as I can remember for falling so far short of the standards my parents, life on a military base, the church, and the directives the teachers have given. Sexual thoughts? Miss church on Sunday? You'll go to hell!

I hate this life.

In recent years, I had also begun resenting my parents for expecting all of this of me. After all, they can't make the cultural or religious grade either. My father drinks too much and stays out late instead of coming home to his wife and kids. And my mom sometimes seems more like a needy child than an adult. Where can I find the mother I need? The father? The two of them are fighting a lot and seem unhappy. It's almost as if they live miles and miles away from one another, and from me and my brother Ron, all inside our picture-perfect suburban home.

I feel torn. I want to follow the path they've given me, but as I observe them struggle with it themselves, I trust this path less and less. Who can I go to for answers? How can I make sense of it all? I feel like everyone else has a road map to life that I haven't been given. As I lie there watching my wrist slowly heal, watching programs like "Leave it to Beaver," I find myself wondering "How come I don't have that?"

By the time I find myself in that hospital bed, recovering from another suicide attempt, I desperately want for my life to change. But getting off drugs and alcohol seems like an impossible task. I had tried so many times and failed. And no one around me has any new ideas, either.

Why even try?

Lesson & Blessing

#1

The Power of Choice

I wasn't *only* a failure. I wasn't *created* as a flawed human being. I was failing at living the typical 1970's American lifestyle. I needed to find other ways to escape the pain of the hypocrisy in the home, church, and country. When I became ready for it many years later, I found the support and love that had always been around me and used it to begin to question my current perspectives, and ultimately change them. This allowed me to make new choices that supported my own life and health, and eventually those around me as well.

This change in outlook and capacity to make life-affirming choices certainly didn't happen overnight. I simply found a first step—then the next, then the next—to getting free from the cycle of self-destruction. For me, the very first step to my current level of freedom was having the experience on the operating table where I chose to stay alive—to *not* leave my body that day in the hospital. This inkling of guidance was powerful and is difficult to explain, but I do know that it created a gateway for more and more of these steps to appear. These choices, over time, started to add up the way snowflakes slowly gather as they fall, eventually blanketing the ground.

The more I observed my life, the more I began making connections between each of my habituated perspectives and the reactive choices I had been making in response to them. These habits had a lot of power since they were all that I had known for so many years. They had literally changed my neurology and biology[2], *and* they were deeply embedded in my family and culture. All of these influences served to reinforce them. In time, I would come to understand that habits are learned behaviors, steeped in addiction, and we *do* have the power to change. Prior to learning this lesson, being unconscious to choice had kept me buried, asleep; but as I began asking questions, I awakened to more of life than the small world in which I lived. I began digging into books and philosophies. I began to break out of the insulated life I had been living and recognize that there's power in the unknown—the power to move mountains, the power to choose and change.

My life caught fire when I realized that I had a choice in how I looked at my life. If I wanted, I could be a

---

[2] See Appendix B

victim. Like so many others, I could recite the wrongs of my childhood over and over like worn out, distorted mantras. Or I could forgive the mistakes of the past, both mine and others', and embrace the fact that I was actually at the cause of my life right now, rather than at the effect. No matter how much pain and sorrow, destruction, or isolation, I now have a choice about how I perceive what had occurred in the past.

But that understanding didn't come easily, and certainly not at age 19, post-second-suicide attempt. First I would have to descend into Hell. Like Dante's "Inferno," I would pass through many layers, going deeper and deeper into suffering and shame, to the point that I felt sure I would never find my way back. For me, Heaven existed, yes, but only as a tiny glimpse through the *Presence* I experienced while on the table, and through recognizing the two women who supported me. Heaven was still a place for someone else... someone I thought I would never know.

The fact that I somehow found my way through the maze of that inferno still awes me to this day. Instead of Hell, I have come to understand it as a crucible, a place where the dross of my old self burns away. This sparked the alchemy of my life. Like William Blake, who wrote of the marriage of Heaven and Hell, I have now learned to bring opposites together, to hold with acceptance both the dark and the light inside myself. Through this *union*, and not the *rejection* of my dark side, I've found true salvation— not an escape from this life, but the joy of moving deeper into its mysteries.

So now we come to the blessing. As I embraced the lesson of *choice*, I began to receive the blessing of *freedom*. With choice came the possibility of knowing *joy*. I moved from a life of addiction and suffering, created by feelings of abandonment, shame, and guilt, into an experience of true connection with Spirit, with other people, and most important, with myself. I define Spirit as the divine living in and through me, the part of me that is already whole and complete, and made in the image and likeness of the Creator.

Out of dark beginnings, I've found my true motto, a self-styled mantra that beats like a drum underneath everything I do: *My life is an answered prayer. My life is an answered prayer. My life is an answered prayer.*

From this expanded understanding, reflecting on the early part of my life is a little like staring into a fun-house mirror. The distorted perspectives that drove my life back then can now make my head swim. But I know I need to share these stories, not to elicit your sympathy, but rather to show that anyone really can get out of Hell. No matter what mistakes you've made, how many times you've made them, or how horrible they seem to you or others around you, you truly do have the power of choice, which can change your life.

I've also finally learned that no road map exists for any of us. A compass, a guidebook, knowledge of the stars— we only have tools, and not a set course for how to make our way home. I know that my experiences may not be the same for you, but I share them because I know that a story holds a special kind of magic. It can inspire hope.

In my early life, hope was probably the hardest thing to come by. I offer it now, with my hand reaching out to yours. You are not alone. The story of my journey to Hell is for you, as well as my ascent from it. May you find your way swiftly to your heaven... more swiftly than I ever did.

Roots

"I wonder how much of what weighs me down

is not mine to carry?"

~ Aditi

"You're expelled," my mom tells me as she comes through the front door, throwing my school books down on the couch.

Expelled. I'm *expelled*?! Shock burns the word into my brain. I'm 12, and I've been at this school for nearly four years now—the longest I've been at any school—and have never even been sent to the Mother Superior's office. How can I possibly be expelled?

Just moments before her devastating news, I'd been having

a rare experience of relishing how much I was enjoying life, finally settled in one place long enough to make some friends. Things seemed the most stable they had been in a *long* time. The sun was throwing its happy arms out over our front yard like an old friend offering me a hug. I was daydreaming about getting back to school the next day where I could see my friends again.

I'd never really felt this way about any place in the world before now. When we'd first arrived nearly four years ago, my Catholic school in Warner Robins, Georgia, had seemed like nothing more than a new flavor of the same old impossible. After the first week, I figured I could add one more to the long list of schools I'd attended where I didn't fit in. In my mind, I'd continually repeated the story that "I am different" and that "all the other students had been together since kindergarten, and they obviously wouldn't want to know me." They also didn't seem to mind the unhappy Irish nuns lurking around every corner, with faces like swollen blisters protruding from too-tight habits. The nuns enforced strict rules and harsh discipline, all the while insisting, "God is Love." Something had definitely felt off to me... but was it them? No, I'd quickly convinced myself that it must have been me.

But eventually time worked some magic. I was finally in one school long enough to put down roots! Gradually, I adjusted to the new school's culture and characters, until one day I realized that I, too, was part of the fabric of the place.

With all of this flooding my mind and the heat still in my body, I sit flabbergasted and plead with Mom, "How can they kick me out like this? Don't they understand how much these people and this place mean to me? Maybe I can make it right somehow... talk to the Mother Superior to apologize and try and to repair my mistake? I mean, Jesus forgave the woman at the well, and I know I haven't done anything so bad as adultery!"

She looks at me with a blank stare as I go on and on asking what I did to upset them. Then she replies coolly, "Now we have to leave here because the school has kicked you out."

The devastation sets in. My secret belief that I'm a defective person has proof. What sin have I committed? I don't know for sure, but this must be my fault. I've done something so bad that even God can't forgive me. After all, a Catholic school has expelled me, so God must be behind this.

Over and over, I try to make it add up in my head, combing my memories for some terrible act. Maybe I said something rude to one of the nuns without realizing it? But the more I think about it, the more tangled and crazy I feel inside. What's the matter with all these mean, old nuns to make them do this to me? What's wrong with this stupid world and its stupid old rules, anyway?

I spend most of that week in a daze, feeling that I don't deserve to be alive.

In truth, my life had begun unraveling long before that awful day. My childhood before Georgia was a whirlwind. We were in constant motion for the first decade. Following my father's career, we crisscrossed the globe. As a military family, this meant that we landed again and again in the world's most politically charged situations. I quickly learned that life is an ever-shifting tumble of places, faces, and expectations, and I could count on no one outside of our nuclear family.

I discovered early on that being sensitive and precocious would win me no favor, so I learned to make myself invisible by withdrawing into my own world. Though not entirely spoken, the expectation was that "children should be seen and not heard."

By the time I was two, our family had already moved from Salina, Kansas, where I had been born, halfway around the world to Tachikawa, Japan. My mother, brother, and I made the journey to join my father, who had arrived before us, on a large boat that took "a month of Sundays" to carry us to this distant place.

Our nanny, Yuka, was a slight Japanese woman with a reserved nature. As a two-year-old, the world was a sensory experience more than a thoughtful one; so through the tones used around me by Mom, and others, the strangeness and hostility of the place was vaguely known to me. Americans living in Japan less than ten years after World War II had ended might be treated politely, but we couldn't expect to be truly welcomed into this culture. Fortunately, Yuka cared for me with genuine warmth. She was a tether for me in this foreign world.

After just two years in Japan, my family moved back to the States. It was 1957 and my maternal grandmother, Evelyn, was dying and needed my mother's care. The military put us in a temporary holding pattern at Chanute Air Force Base in Illinois so we could be with her.

My relationship with my grandmother began to take a different shape than my mother's, who didn't understand her own mother's strong entrepreneurial nature and independence. Even without many words yet in my vocabulary, I understood my grandmother almost instantly, as though I was finally meeting a kindred spirit. I played with a box of animal crackers together with her in her hospital bed, getting to know each animal and their sounds intimately. Her presence felt safe and familiar to me, even though I'd spent so little time with her.

I wouldn't know this comfort for long. Later that year, she died. We stayed at Chanute for another year or so before, once again, Dad got transferred, this time into the charged atmosphere of Cold War Germany. While he got set up there, the three of us moved to Pennsylvania for a few months where I started kindergarten, before joining Dad overseas once again.

It was 1959 and the country was only just beginning to heal from the trauma of World War II. Tensions ran high between German locals and American military personnel posted there as we watched the Berlin Wall rise across the landscape over the next two years.

Again I found myself far from relatives or family friends, dealing with a new place and culture unlike any before it. At least I had my family. I had my daddy.

My father would sometimes brag that he had been "quite the catch" in his youth. My aunts—his four sisters—had all doted on him since he was the only boy left in the family, as their favorite older brother had died in a car accident on his 30th birthday (the same day my brother Ron was born!). My aunties would tell me that Dad's good looks made him popular with the ladies, and that he was a "man's man" at heart—the strong, silent type who liked to hang out at the bar with his buddies.

He told us that he'd enlisted in the military on his 16th birthday. This only increased his appeal to women, since a uniform still carried with it a healthy dose of respect in the mid-1940's. But being enlisted would come to mean so much more than flirtatious glances from pretty girls. In ways I suspect he couldn't have imagined as a teenager, his role in the military would shape everything about his life, and eventually, our family's life, too.

By the time we moved to Germany, Dad was in his early thirties and in great shape. This good-looking soldier would leave our house every morning in green army fatigues, with black stripes on his arms and tall black boots laced a few inches above his ankles. In the evenings, he switched into khaki pants and a clean white t-shirt. With a beer in his hand, he would lie back in his favorite reclining chair and watch TV. Alcohol seemed to take the edge off of things for him. And as long as he stayed functional in his life, no one questioned his drinking. To me, it was normal.

Actually, no one questioned my father about anything, at least not in our home. Dad ruled the roost. He was a military man who had traveled up the ranks, and he was used to barking orders to men who jumped at his call. He expected us—his family—to behave the same way. We all tiptoed around him, my mother in charge of keeping the peace. "Stay out of your father's way," she would mumble under her breath to one of us as she quietly crossed through the room. "He's had a hard day."

My mother would also often say to me, "Don't tell your father," about any number of things—the money we spent, something she let me do, or anything that might rile him up. I quickly adopted her way of keeping secrets so as not to rock the boat. While we were in Germany, he didn't spend much time at the house, but when he did show up, I would read his mood by finding out whether or not he wanted to talk. I relished the times when he would grab me to play. Dad always smelled fresh and clean, like Old Spice and Prell shampoo—except when he drank too much. I hated the day-after stench that hung around him. I knew when he'd been drinking before I smelled him, though, because I would wake up to a mess on the kitchen stove where he had made something to eat during the night.

"You're father's had a few too many," Mom would say as she quietly cleaned up his mess. Something about it made my skin crawl.

Each Sunday, Mom would lay me on the kitchen counter with my head over the sink to wash my hair. Then she rolled it while we all watched "Bonanza" or "The Ed Sullivan Show." Mom and Dad played lots of records at home, everything from Big Band to Elvis Presley to Hank Williams. I learned a love of dancing from my mother. Sometimes our whole family spent Sunday afternoon at the NCO Club, where they had dances for kids with twisting contests to Chubby Checker's tunes. Sometimes I even won!

I was only just starting to understand the difference in status between us, the kids of the non-commissioned officers who have enlisted, and the kids of the officers who have college degrees. I noticed that their houses look nicer than ours, but I made friends with these kids as easily as any, and the differences between us didn't bother me much.

During this time, my sensitivity started becoming apparent to the people around me. I would know things about other people, often before my parents did. Things that no one had told me. I just sensed things, the way I could feel the wind blow.

One day, a friend of my parents came over, and I began talking about private aspects of the person's life that I couldn't have known without someone telling me. Everyone in the room was taken aback, especially this friend. How could I have known his secrets? This strange psychic ability was both a gift and a curse. But as a child, this didn't seem strange or extraordinary to me. It felt as natural as talking and walking.

Of course, my parents weren't exactly thrilled with my ability. It made me unpredictable. Someone my father worked with but hardly knew might drop in at our house, only for me to start up a conversation with him about what was going on with his wife as though I knew all the details of his life. Without anyone telling me, I could feel his pain, sense his suffering.

To put me in my place, my parents began calling me *Miss Missileer*, the title of the newspaper on the air force base. This name implied I might announce the news of the day at any minute, dragging out of the closet the skeletons people most wanted tucked safely out of sight.

My parents saw their teasing as good-natured. It helped them put a little distance between themselves and the uncanny ability I had to grasp the unspoken and give it words. But the name left me feeling powerless. I was only five years old, but already my strengths were proving a liability.

In 1963 at 9 years old, we once again moved back to the States. I couldn't call it home, since I'd spent less of my life in this country than I had abroad. My father was stationed at Robins Air Force Base in Georgia, where I found myself surrounded by every race, creed, color, and class, just as I always had—military life in Japan and Germany had always put us in the middle of highly diverse populations.

This time, though, racial unrest was tearing through the countryside just past our fence line. I watched footage of race riots on TV, but this conflict wasn't happening somewhere far away. For the first time in my life, I encountered, in Warner Robins, public bathrooms, drinking fountains, and seating marked either "Colored" or "White." At first, I couldn't even comprehend what the signs meant. Skin color had never borne any weight. When my parents explained them to me, I was flabbergasted, confused. Here I was, still a child, with no real understanding of what the heck was going on around me. I felt like I was on a merry-go-round going much too fast, and my head began spinning.

I felt myself pulled among a hundred worlds at once. Where did I fit in any of them?

And still, I looked to my father as my rock. As things changed around us, I teased and joked with him. I was his baby girl, his princess. Even if I didn't know anyone at school or where I would live next year, I knew I mattered to someone.

I was 11—three years into my time at the Catholic school—when my father received deployment orders to a new duty station, not for another base in the States or even somewhere overseas where we could go with him. This time, he was going to Thailand in service to America and the Vietnam War.

Before this, the war in Vietnam seemed more like a movie than something real. Each night, I sat on the floor between my mother's legs as she rolled my hair, this time both of us watching the news of what was happening in that tiny country far away, rather than the evening entertainment. To me, anything on the TV was happening to *other* people, on the *other* side of the cameras just the same as people appearing on "The Ed Sullivan Show."

But now, my father was going to be leaving us. My father who doted on me, his only daughter. The nightly news could soon be talking about him. I tucked away another secret fear.

After I learned that he would be leaving, I took in those news programs with totally different eyes. Bombs going off, people fighting and dying in Vietnam... a jumble of painful emotions twisted inside me. Something was coming, a big change. I could feel it.

Since family members couldn't live on base while enlisted personnel go on tour, our family moved into a brand-new, brick, two-bedroom apartment about two miles away. This was the first time I'd lived off of a military base in many, many years. I felt lost and alone once again.

Not long before my father was going to ship out, I went into my new bedroom, where two single beds, perfectly made just as Dad insisted—one for me and one for Ron—took up most of the space in the mostly empty room. I pulled the door closed behind me.

Outside, gray clouds filled the sky, making the room around me feel heavy and dull. On the inside, I felt thunderheads building. I longed to crack myself open the same way jagged shards of lightning could tear open a Georgia summer sky. Maybe then all this inner turmoil I kept carefully locked inside me could wash away.

"Daddy, please don't go!" I wanted to say, to shout. But the words still lived in my throat, stuck like a wad of cotton. So many words were crammed up in there. I wanted to ask him, "Will you come back alive?" I wanted to tell him, "Daddy, I'm scared. Please come back alive, please."

But I couldn't get any of the feelings of confusion to come out. My mind was locked down in prison, solitary confinement. After all, my job was to smile and be a brave little girl for both of my parents.

Feeling helpless, I lied on the floor and pushed up underneath one leg of my single bed. I put my left arm underneath it, then dropped the bed on my arm. The whole weight of the wooden bed frame came crashing down on my small bones.

What was I doing? I didn't know. But I did it again, then again, repeatedly dropping the bed on my own arm. Pain screamed through me, almost more than I could bear. But at least I could finally feel *something*. This physical pain spoke volumes about everything inside me that I couldn't put into words.

At the hospital, x-rays revealed a fractured arm. I lied and told my parents that I had fallen out of a tree. I couldn't bear for them to know what I had done; I couldn't even really admit it to myself. Couldn't they see how messed up everything was about to get? The pain in my body seemed like the only voice I had to get their attention.

It was Easter Sunday, a few days before my father was leaving for his one-year tour. I stood next to him, my man-god, in front of the brick facade, and smiled for our family photo, just like he told me. My arm was in a cast. And I pretended everything was alright.

But when Dad left, whatever had been normal about my life evaporated. My brother Ron escaped the madhouse by going to live at a Catholic minor seminary for boys. My mother continued working, now more than ever, and used this as her personal escape and refuge, leaving me by myself in our apartment for long stretches at a time.

I was now going it alone.

One day, only a few months before I was expelled, I realized that my mother, a woman who yearns for love from my father, was having an affair with the father of one of my friends. I knew this was a mortal sin—the Catholic church says so—and the thought of it devastated me. But I had no one to talk to about it, and no place to turn.

One evening she came home from work and I confronted her. We were standing in the small, narrow hallway between our bedrooms, my face close to hers. "I'm pissed off at you!" I yelled, my words like a whip cracking the air.

Shock spread over my mother's face. How did I know? How had her daughter found out about the affair? I watched these questions

cross her face in milliseconds, then vanish behind her swooping hand as it slapped my face.

Next, shock hit me, even harder than my mother's hand. She had never raised a hand against me before this instant. I lifted my own hand to the red sting on my cheek.

Yes, I knew these words, "pissed off," are a big deal in 1966—off-limits curse words that no young lady should use. But this was the only way to express the hurt that knots my gut. Yet, how dare she hit me!

At that moment, I built the wall. And my mother belonged on the other side of it. From now on, she would be East Berlin and I would be West. I shut her out of my life, punishing her without words.

Not too long after, we received the good news! Dad was coming home. He'd be stationed in southern New Mexico where we would join him back on base. Over the phone, I heard my mother tell Dad that she wants Ron and me to finish school with our current class before we join him there. But I knew the truth. She wanted more time with her new man.

And now, I'm expelled and Mom tells me we have to leave because of it. My mind is whirling so fast with thoughts building like a tornado at an accelerating speed, getting ready to swoop down and further wreck my world. After the self-blame quiets down a little, something deep down inside—that psychic capacity I'd developed early on—knows that my mother's affair had been the reason for the nuns' decision to get rid of me.

The pressure from the situation at school, along with her desire to stay longer in Georgia, forces Mom to tell Dad about what she's been up to.

By the time he comes back from Thailand, Dad has worked himself into a fury. For a year, he's been a part of one of the most brutal, four-year wars in history. Now he's finally returned, but to what? My mother's affair has blown up his idea of home like a bomb in one of Vietnam's rice fields.

I blame myself for his anger. I can't stop thinking about how I'd gotten expelled and disgraced our whole family. And underneath it all, I boil with silent tension knowing that Mom's affair was also at play. The overwhelming hurt brought on from all this has me so confused—do I love her or build the wall higher so I can't be hurt any further? Do I care for Dad's hurt feelings or protect Mom from his fury? How do I get out of here like Ron has?

Before Dad left for the war, I'd inhabited our family's world as Daddy's precious girl. He lavished me with nicknames like Tea Waddle, Po'Dunkin, and Loula Bell. But all this has also now changed. I rack my brain trying to put my finger on how it had started. Had his trip to Thailand set this in motion? My mother's affair? My expulsion from Sacred Heart Catholic School? No matter what had prompted it, I now know one thing for sure: A new war has begun, and it's happening in my family and inside my own head. Would we ever feel the love between us again?

When I see him again, he calls me "Loula Bell," mussing my hair playfully. For a fleeting instant, I become Daddy's Little Princess again and catch a glimpse of that love. But the moment fades quickly. Before long, the arguments commence between my mother and father, and I feel like I'm going crazy again, blaming myself for all of it.

All these changes are taking a toll on me. And now we're moving yet again. This time to the foreign land of the southern New Mexican desert. On the verge of puberty, I find myself more and more angry at my parents, myself, and the world. I'm not acting like the sweet little girl my father had known when he left. Before long, that innocent girl is gone for good.

Lesson & Blessing

#2

Cultural Conditioning

As children and young adults, we see our parents as the gatekeepers of our lives. They are authority figures. They are caregivers. But to us, they aren't yet truly human. We can't even imagine that our parents had also gone to school, fallen in love, and struggled with making friends, much less comprehend that they had parents of their own who were, in turn, affected by experiences with their parents, in their cultural context.

In my early life, I couldn't see my mother as someone who had once been a child. For me, she had always been a mother. This is childhood. We swim in a sea of innocent narcissism with only ourselves at its center, not as a mis- guided perspective but as a natural part of development. In the long run, however, this way of seeing and thinking can set us up for a fair amount of confusion. Just as we believe we're the center of the world, we also hold ourselves as the source of all of its problems—"I'm the reason Dad is so an- gry now; it's all my fault." Or, "I'm the reason Mom is never happy anymore."

Long past childhood, these self-beliefs become the habitual ways in which we beat ourselves up. Throughout so many years of my life I felt guilty for both my and my family's mistakes. Not until later, when I began reflecting more on my early life with more clarity, could I see how much my childhood experiences had shaped me, and not only for the worse. And not only some of my experiences. All of them. The events in my family impacted me. The attitudes at my church and school affected me. Even the larger social climate that surrounded me, events like the aftermath of World War II, the erection of the Berlin Wall, the Cold War, and the race riots in Georgia. All of these had an influence on how I would relate to the world as an adult.

Throughout my childhood, I moved in and out of such a wide range of climates. I don't only mean the frequently changing scenery outside my door, either. I also constantly had to maneuver through new internal landscapes. What psyche ruled each place? How did people from this locale judge the rest of the world? After witnessing so many different cultural perspectives, I also wanted to know which one was *real*? If my family served as my anchor, then I can see why I felt so anchor-less. These people I called my family were also struggling through life, each as confused and lost as I was.

Everyone in my family felt some version of the loneliness that swept over me when Dad got orders to go to Thailand. All of us dealt with it in our own ways, with our own versions of crying out for help. For me, it had been breaking my arm and yelling at Mom. For Mom, it had been the affair. And my brother had gotten the role of the "good boy," escaping the chaos of our family by going to seminary.

From the outside, our family looked relatively normal. My parents had good jobs, put us in good schools, and ushered us to church on Sundays. We were doing everything right. But deep inside it all felt wrong.

For many years, I felt a flood of tangled emotions

about that first decade of my life. In fact, I wouldn't even be able to *begin* to understand the impact of these experiences until I reached my thirties, well into addiction recovery. In the beginning, it came down to a few essential realizations: I needed love. I wanted attention. I wanted a mother who didn't have affairs and a father who didn't leave me behind for work and alcohol. I wanted to fit into the prevailing attitude of the 1950's: "Don't do as I do, do as I say."

To deal with the pain that these yearnings caused, I'd chosen to break my own arm. As I got older, I often cut myself and controlled my eating, imagining that at least I had control over *something*. I was trying to move the hurt out of me. Back then, no one spoke openly about such things, and I felt certain that I was the only one experiencing these shame-filled behaviors.

Fortunately, these behaviors are now being well researched and understood, as well as spoken about more publicly, which indicates to me how similar—not different—we all really are.

I don't remember exactly when I started to realize my mother had once been a little girl, then a teenager, then a young woman with yearnings and desires of her own. She was born in a different era, with different social expectations that had shaped her outlook and the way she related to life.

But she felt many of the same pressures as I had, and she also hadn't been given the road map to life.

My mother's relationship with my grandmother had been complex. My grandmother had bucked every social rule by divorcing her husband in 1939 and becoming an independent female entrepreneur. The impact on my mother of losing contact with her father at an early age when everyone around her had both parents, affected her deeply. She had always longed for love and affection that my father didn't know how to give. Given the intensity of the reliance I had on my father as my rock, I can imagine what a huge loss this would have been for my mom.

Yet at the time I was becoming a young woman, I had no idea how walling my mom out would warp my whole life. I couldn't yet understand that shutting her out meant shutting out all the love she had to offer, along with the pain. I had no idea I was walling out not just my mother but life itself. All I knew in the moment of cussing her out was that I wouldn't let her hurt me again.

In time, I came to see that both of my parents had been shaped by their own era, just as I had. Born in the late 1920's and early 1930's, they had tried to live up to the strict gender roles and ethical standards of that time. In those days, most parents saw the task of instilling strict rules for their children as their first and most important duty. Love took a backseat, known by the parent but not usually expressed. Nurturing came as an afterthought, if at all. Could I expect from my parents what they had never received themselves? Even more to the point, how would I have felt to be them, from their era and experiences, trying to deal with a daughter with behaviors like mine? No matter what mistakes they had made, I knew I'd been no picnic for them.

As a rule, their generation married young. In keeping with this cultural expectation, my parents hadn't known each other long when they tied the knot. Children came not long after. When I think of myself at their age with two small children to care for, I understand their generation's many jokes about "the old ball and chain" and other sour euphemisms for a wife or marriage. They had committed their whole lives to a relative stranger, with no option for exit.

The more I could see the connections between my parents' personal histories and their cultural contexts—alcohol abuse, gambling, infidelity, religious zealousness, low-income—and the way they raised me, the easier it became for me to understand what had transpired in our family and why I'd made the choices I made as a response to these conditions. I reflected and realized that the events I witnessed had influenced my perspective on life, so surely my parents' backgrounds had a similar effect in their lives, and so on through our ancestry.

Ultimately, I came to see these early life experiences not as a liability, but a gift for my growth and evolution as a human. My parents and I had been learning this thing called life together, in a way, making it up as we went along.

This, then, was both the lesson *and* blessing from my childhood: understanding that we are naturally shaped by our culture and life experiences, as are the previous generations. And this understanding opened up my life to a whole new kind of freedom, one I never knew I could experience. The conditions in which we grow up aren't a curse, but a blessing... when we begin to see that life isn't happening *to* us, but *for* us.

I share this with you to invite you to explore the humanity of your culture... your parents and family... of everyone in your life. Though it may seem easier to blame them for your struggles, what do you notice when you pause and reflect on the context within which *they* were raised—the influences on their early life choices?

I'm now a student of etymology and love to look up words. Condition means simply *"the state of something with regard to its appearance, quality, or working order."*

As I enter the conditions of new cultures in my life presently, I simply observe the state of things. What do I see? What qualities do I sense are present? What's working well here, and what challenges are here to offer a gateway to growth?

Descent into Hell

"The depth of darkness to which you can descend and still live is an exact measure of the height to which you can aspire to reach."
~ *Pliny the Elder*

We're parked in the desert, the red-orange-yellow-pink of a Southern New Mexico sunset all around us. The cool kids come here on Saturday nights to blow off steam—the *older* cool kids, I mean. The oldest ones in the crowd are pulling beer bottles from crumpled paper sacks, handing them around the group.

How much I want to impress them, both to be like, and be liked by, this group. When a pause in the conversation gives me an opening, I tell a story about how I'd been born a twin but my sister had died in the delivery room. The lie makes me break into a nervous little laugh... a child's imaginative attempt to make her life seem more interesting.

"Wanna have a beer?" a handsome high school junior asks me, holding out an open bottle.

Do I want a beer? Hell, yeah, I do. The soft desert breeze lifts my hair around my face as I reach for the bottle. In every direction, the multi-color sky brightens to blood red, then fades to orange and finally gold as the sun dips below the mesa. My troubles live miles away from here. Besides, I'm big enough now to make my own choices, and I'm ready for my first swig of that liquid cool.

I tip the bottle back. Warmth tickles my tongue, then slides like velvet fire down my throat. Tiny rivers of wet gold spread through me, massaging every nerve ending in my body. Suddenly, I feel. But what is this feeling? It's so unfamiliar, so difficult to describe. A hum spreads through me, the seduction with a thousand tiny arms, cradling and comforting me, softening the jagged edges of my world. For one glorious, perfect moment, I feel whole.

What is this stuff? How is it possible for *anything* to make me feel like this? I had just taken one sip of alcohol to fit in with the kids. But who even cares about what they think about me now? I feel as free as if I'm being let out of jail.

Before I take another sip, the world goes blank. I don't mean that I don't have words for what happens next. No, I actually become a human camera, but one without any film. No part of me remains in my body to record the click, click, click of my life moving past. I'm talking and laughing with the other kids, or so they think. But *I'm* not actually there talking or laughing. I've blacked out.

Finally, I've come home, not to my family, but to whatever this stuff is in the bottle. I'm only 12 years old and I've taken my first drink. At the end of the evening, I arrive back to our military-assigned apartment and go to sleep. The best sleep I've had in years.

Here at the new base, plenty of people recognize us as a lovely family. But I see my father drinking now more than ever. And he's not just yelling at my mother anymore but at me, too—calling me a whore, a bitch, a slut. Sometimes his anger turns physical, leaving me with bruises. The pain of his marital betrayal while away serving his country has gotten to him, and he's taking it out on me in new ways— not only by belittling me, but now with physical beatings. Fighting has become a way of life in our household. Now that we're in New Mexico, Ron had to come with us, and he finds more reasons to stay away from home to avoid what he has no power to control.

I'd already given up on church and God in Georgia. What kind of God would force me to get expelled because of my mother's mistakes? What kind of church does this to an innocent child? As a military kid with no close ties to family or friends, I have no one to confide in about the pain I'd gone through by abruptly leaving my old school or the fear over my father's increased drinking. Why aren't we like the Cleaver family on TV? I'm certain that everyone else but me has a wholesome family.

In a big, bad, confusing world, I feel alone.

What a relief, in the midst of all of this madness, to find the haven of that cool, calming drink. All I have to do is lift a bottle to my mouth, and for the first time in my life, I feel at ease. So simple. Another sip and I feel comfortable in my body. It's okay now, this whole being alive thing. What good fortune to stumble upon this solution to all my pain. I don't care so much about the alcohol itself. I just want—no, I need—this feeling it gives me.

The next day, I have only a vague trace of a memory from the previous night. How much had I drunk? What had I said, done? How did I get home? Everything after that first bottle had evaporated.

I feel lucky to have discovered the miracle of booze. I knew my parents lied to *each other*, so who might be lying to *me*? In a world full of people I can't trust, at least I can now count on alcohol. And it begins opening doors for me socially too. If it isn't *curing* my problems, at least I get a temporary reprieve from them. For a moment, however transient, I can escape from almost anything, into the warm haze of a good buzz.

Along with alcohol, I experiment with other things, too. Back in Georgia, I had begun letting boys fondle me. Good girls didn't do this, and I knew it. I had to save myself for marriage. So I walked as close to this edge as I could without crossing over into completely forbidden territory.

Through these sexual encounters I finally feel like I'm getting some attention. Naively, I believe that a boy won't do something like this unless he cares about me, and of course I really want for someone to care. "You're a loose girl," the church says in one ear every time I let a boy touch me. And in the other ear, I hear some part of me saying, "But this feels good, and he must love me."

In New Mexico, my now growing interest in both alcohol and boys increases the tension at home. One day I come home the morning after another night of drinking and my dad immediately lays into me, asking "Where have you been?" "I don't know," I reply, and he and Mom assume I'm lying. This triggers more verbal and physical abuse. The reality is that I actually don't know where I'd been. The drinking and amnesia are linked, but I don't tell them my secret. I simply enjoy the feeling of that cool liquid making its way into my body each time.

Much to my father's dismay, his little Loula Bell is gone.

Of course, I don't tell my father that I've discovered drinking. He's a stern, military man who has gone from being intimidating to downright frightening since we moved to Holloman Air Force Base. He would never guess that a 12-year-old would be drinking anyway. But he can tell something is wrong with me. He just doesn't know what. So Dad does the only thing he knows and puts me on "restriction," a state I begin living in. It's like being grounded, but worse. On restriction, I can't leave the house; I'm assigned a long list of daily chores, with no going out on the weekend, no TV, and an imperative to be home directly after school. As I struggle with the militarist rules Dad tries to instill, Ron disappears to avoid it all. I see him out riding his scooter, playing baseball, mowing lawns, and staying away from home more and more. I can't say I blame him. I feel disconnected from his world as my world gets crazier and crazier.

Naturally, I find ways around my father's strict rules. And when I find one, it usually involves drinking. Then I don't come home at all. When I eventually resurface, I don't know where I've been or why I can't explain what's happened. And the next punishment commences. When I'm on restriction, I replay the hurtful, angry words my father spews over and over in my head, punishing myself even before the next blow he doles out, coming to believe that I deserve it.

I disappear more and more, and my parents are becoming more angry and upset. The first half dozen times I go missing, they call the police, who can't find me. Each time they bring in the police, my father is called into his Commanding Officer's office and reprimanded. It's expected that he keeps his family in line, and when he's unable to do so, he gets desperate to control me.

This scenario continues to play out over the course of a year or so, and alcohol begins to take more from me than it gives. Alcohol that had once made me feel so good starts to pull me down. I'm now beginning to experience a depth of shame that has me needing to kill that pain also. My 13-year-old reality is being completely shaped by the traps of alcohol.

For that entire year, anytime I have a chance, I chase the feeling of that first drink. But somehow it keeps eluding me, a little more every time. The weight of the world begins to creep over me, like vines choking out a garden. *Who am I? What is the point of any of this? Are pain and emptiness the only things I have to look forward to?*

Living on base, I stand at ground zero. My father never talks with us about his experiences in Thailand or in the Vietnam War. But the men on base talk at the Airman's Club Cafeteria, where I'm hanging out, so I get a glimpse of the controversy of the war. A sense of the connection I once felt between me and my family members is now present in these men's stories rather than over the dinner table or hair-washing at the sink.

A year after we arrive in New Mexico, I find myself sitting in one man's tiny apartment, a tapestry over one door, a beaded curtain hanging over the other. Conversations about the war bloom in little patches around the room—what's it all for? Why are people dying over this thing? What does life really mean, anyway? In the background, "White Rabbit" by Jefferson Airplane and hints of marijuana fill the air.

I'm drinking that night, feeling like I'm part of the group, and don't even think about my family. I pass out and wake up the next morning in shock to discover that once again, I haven't made it home. The terror immediately washes over me as I think about Dad's rage, mixed with no recollection of the events of the night before. When I finally arrive home later that day, my father beats me with both his belt *and* his fists this time.

So, when I take a whole bottle of aspirin later that morning, I follow it with more alcohol I had stashed in my room. I want the pain to end—the pain of disappointing my family and myself. The pain of keeping too many secrets... too many unspoken thoughts and feelings. Even though I'm trying to kill myself, I don't yet really understand the finality of death. I just want out.

I arrive at the hospital, once again with no recollection of the previous events. My tiny body requires the doctor to find a vein in my ankle to treat me as they pump my stomach. Nurses check me into the pediatric ward once I'm stable. Despite all posturing and posing as a grown-up, I'm still a child—one who's just tried to take her own life.

Before the medical team finishes with me, they have one more exam to perform. Because I'd been partying overnight with young airmen, my father instructs them to check me to see if I'm still a virgin. They conduct this exam in silence, without a word of explanation.

My sexuality, already a source of complicated feelings, becomes a tangle of unspeakable pain before the doctors complete this test. I'm alone realizing that my virginity is in question, knowing inside that I'm still a virgin. I'd never before been invaded in this way, and I'm mortified, confused. Ashamed beyond words.

When they check me out of the hospital several days later, my parents tell me that they've found a psychiatrist in Ft. Bliss, Texas, a full 50 miles from our house. That is 50 long, painful miles of car time with my parents, the wind whipping tumbleweeds across the highway the entire way there. Their disappointment in me forms a second, invisible wind that whips through every crevice of my life. It scatters my thoughts like papers blown across a road. It howls through the tunnels of my sleep, keeping me lost in nightmares that lead to hours of tossing and turning. It pushes me toward an edge I can sense, even if I can't see it. Getting expelled had been mortifying. But this is a hundred—a thousand times—worse. I'm not only a rebellious teen, I now consider myself crazy.

I try my best to pretend their disappointment doesn't matter to me by becoming more tough and cool every day. But under my brittle surface, a terrified little girl is still yearning for her parents' love. Their disappointment in me matters; it matters a lot. But what can I do? Daddy's Little Princess has turned into a monster.

Inside me, anger begins turning to rage. Am I crazy? Maybe everyone else is crazy. I mean, everything feels crazy to me—the crazy Vietnam War, my crazy dad hitting me, the crazy church that had kicked me out because of my crazy mom's stupid mistake. But most of all, I feel crazy inside, like a ball of knotted up yarn. The more I work to untangle the thing, the more knotted up I become. I can't think straight. I can't find my way through this mess. But I make the drive in silence. I have no words to explain my bizarre behavior.

The psychiatrist is an older man, maybe 40, peering over his glasses at me. I sit down in a big black leather chair. My feet don't touch the floor, dangling as I stare past the man. So serious. Intense. He's certainly going to get to the bottom of my problems.

But of course, he doesn't.

And neither does the next one, nor the next. I'm an Air Force kid. I know the rules. You aren't supposed to talk about your family, not ever. These doctors ask me questions and without obvious, scripted answers to respond to them, I believe they're merely setting traps. I'm not going to tell those doctors shit even if I had a mouthful of it.

So I keep quiet. One doctor's chair is pretty much like the next. My legs get longer, my hairstyle changes. I add more makeup. But I endure each new psychiatrist with the same stoic silence. If I do speak, I make sure not to reveal anything. These doctors become a part of the scenery; furniture in the world I'd already decided to wall out forever when Mom first slapped me. I can't trust them any more than I can her.

And even if I *could* trust them, even if I had someone—just one person in my life to whom I could confide my secrets—what would I say? Where would I even begin? By now, everything is so mixed up inside me, like too many paint colors running together into an ugly purple/brown, the color of a deep bruise. Everything feels tender. Raw. Nothing makes sense anymore.

Nothing, that is, except for the obvious: I'm the problem. If I'd doubted that truth before, well, I can't doubt it now. I'm seeing psychiatrists, I'm losing track of chunks of time that I can't explain or remember, and I'd tried to kill myself. No matter how crazy my family members seem to me, I now have them all beat.

Lesson & Blessing

#3

Scapegoat Magic

Looking back, I can't even say how much I was drinking, but I imagine it didn't take much for my little, 76-pound body to feel the effects of booze. That time in my life reminds me of a paper snowflake. Alcohol cut holes through every part of my experience. But at 12, I had no idea that it could do something like that. And over time, I suspected my brain had damage that no one could repair, which propelled me to keep using it to calm my nerves and provide a much-needed escape.

At such a young age, my brain was still coming out of childhood. My prefrontal cortex, that part of the brain we use to make judgment calls, hadn't yet developed. Unlike an adult, I didn't have the capacity to keep the urge to drink in check. If this sounds like an excuse, consider the fact that a person who doesn't become a smoker before age 21 will probably never become addicted to nicotine[3]. By then, the prefrontal cortex has matured, and life has shown you enough

---

[3] Fatma Romeh M. Ali, PhD, "Onset of Regular Smoking Before Age 21 and Subsequent Nicotine Dependence and Cessation Behavior Among US Adult Smokers"

to know that the instant of pleasure from a cigarette will never balance out the hurt the habit could cause.

On top of this, research[4] has shown that people vary in their ability to make a solid judgment call and keep impulses in check. Conditions like anxiety and depression directly affect this variability. With these, a person—*on a cellular level*—has much less stamina for making sound personal decisions. And he or she will be more susceptible to the pull of addiction due to low levels of neurotransmitters like serotonin, which addictive substances can temporarily boost.

From this perspective, I was dealing with a stacked deck with that first drink in my hand at age 12. A family history of alcoholism, combined with an undeveloped brain, hormonal changes, and the depression and anxiety I felt over my crumbling family life, meant that I was easy prey for addiction's seductive snare.

None of this stuff excuses me from responsibility for my choices. But it does help me understand why drinking seemed like such a good idea to me back then. My body, not just my mind, craved this substance. That same mind had no filters to warn me about impending consequences, either.

Writing about how I became an alcoholic feels like looking at a sepia photograph of an unfamiliar relative. Who was

---

[4]   Howard J. Shaffer, PhD, CAS, "What is Addiction?"

that person, the angry girl who had no words, no trust, no use for life? I've logged decades of recovery since 1979 without alcohol and drugs, and I barely recall seeing the world through the lens of this 12 year-old girl.

Yet more than once, well-meaning friends and acquaintances have asked me, "Linda, you have so much time sober now. Don't you think it would be okay to have a drink every now and then?"

My answer comes easy: "Why would anyone want just one drink?"

That's the one way I know that some part of me remains as the girl who reached for alcohol to survive. I never cared about alcohol, per se. I was chasing the feeling alcohol gave me in that first drink.

So now when I look back at myself, I'm overwhelmed with compassion for the lost little girl who found a strategy to feel belonging. That first encounter with booze gave me the first moment of relief I'd experienced since my family began to unravel.

In my unconscious choice to use booze as a way of gaining some sense of sanity, I hadn't been alone. We were a lost generation. We were growing up on baseball and apple pie, on smiling women in crisply starched dresses and perfect makeup who greeted their kind, thoughtful husbands at their doors. None of that was preparing us for the actuality of the world we were facing. The same TV sets that brought us "Gidget," "The Flying Nun," and "Mr. Ed" also delivered real-life horror stories into our living rooms every night with the Vietnam War. We suffered from emotional whiplash, wandering through the wreckage of what our world had become.

"Don't trust anyone over 30" was our motto, forged in the fallout of events like Watergate, race riots, and Vietnam. Even now, my father doesn't talk about what he experienced during his time serving during that war. He, too, felt disoriented, overwhelmed by the events of the era. The rules of his own generation no longer worked, but he had no models for how to parent me in a new way and no faith in the wife who had betrayed him. His anger left my mother feeling more alone than ever.

The mounting pressure in my family needed an escape valve. Me!

I understand now that I served as my family's scapegoat, acting out the pent up emotions that all of us were feeling but couldn't express. As a sensitive kid, I both felt the tension the most *and* had the least tolerance for it. I turned all that unexpressed strain into wild, unpredictable behavior, which made me—not the shared, buried pain—the focal point of the family's troubles. By acting out, I carried the weight for us all.

When I reach back through time for this younger version of myself, I do so with great tenderness. I see now that I wasn't the problem in my family. I was responding to the best of my ability to a complex web of troubles much bigger than only my parents and their challenges and mistakes. We had all gotten stuck together in the web of *their* parents' unresolved issues, the pain of a nation at war, and ultimately, the sadness and heartbreak of a whole world trying to find its way. That younger Linda made some poor choices, yes. But who had shown her anything different?

And in that compassion, I hold a paradox. I didn't cause the chaos around me. But even if I didn't choose my situation, I still had choices. I created my experience of these circumstances through my attitude toward them.

I bore not blame, but responsibility for my life. Even for the poor choices I made, I don't blame myself. Rather, I own what I did. Taking responsibility for these choices gives me access to something priceless: my personal power.

When I became aware of this dynamic in our family many years later and began to shift the cycle through recovery, I no longer served as the focal point of all of our collective problems. Each member of the family then began to feel the effects of their own behaviors. It created discomfort as they were no longer able to use me as their scapegoat.

The blessing in disguise at the time of the onset of my drinking is now more recognizable as a true blessing, as the pressure that had been solely on me now had its right place in the wider family system.

If you've ever been the scapegoat, then you know how tough it can be to hear that you're the problem, and then that you also need to take responsibility for yourself. After all, everyone else is already pointing a finger at you. Why do they get to be right? On the other hand, I learned something powerful in later years about scapegoat magic. As the scapegoat, I'd given my family an excuse to ignore their own faults and traumas, which allowed them to ignore the real issues at hand. But as the focal point of their attention, I would spark our collective transformation through the example of my own recovery.

Committed

"Sometimes the only way to stay sane
is to go a little crazy."
~Susanna Kaysen, "Girl, Interrupted"

I n love. I'm in love.

This isn't a boy fondling me in the bathroom at school. This isn't a crush. I'm now 17, old enough to be thinking of marriage. And Steve has already told me he'll never let anything happen to me. I feel so safe with him, finally cared for and seen after being alone for so long. I know I've found the real thing. True love.

And who wouldn't fall in love with this guy? Gentle and kind, this tall, blond farm boy with blue eyes stands out in a crowd. A life-time of physical labor has nicely enhanced his strapping build, which hints at Scandinavian or Swedish roots. In his free time, he channels all that physical energy into a drum and bugle corps, which calls for long hours of both musical practice and physical exertion. But this commitment only seems to strengthen, not tire, him. Steve's country-boy good manners and clean-cut good looks clear a space in the world that I feel lucky to fill.

My budding relationship with Steve feels like living under a beam of sunshine, and I'm the happiest I can ever remember be-ing in my entire life. He and I double date a lot with my best friend, Lana, who is dating Steve's best friend, Tom. Weekends find us eating hamburgers at the Dog n' Suds, making out to a romance film at the drive-in movies, or hanging out together at a house party, where social drinking is a natural part of the festivities. Steve and his friends have already started college, and I'm a senior in high school. At this age, alcohol seems socially appropriate, if not yet legal for us.

Most of his friends can handle their liquor better than I can, however. What had happened to me? I still can't find the words for it. But I sense, even if I can't explain it to myself, that alcohol is affecting me more than it does other people, or in a different way somehow.

At least I know Steve loves me. We've already had sex, which I seem to have no problems with any longer. I mean, clearly we're meant for each other. In just a few months, I'll graduate high school, Steve college. And I hear wedding bells.

Who wouldn't, though? Lana and her boyfriend are going

steady, and the future looks bright for them. Our parents haven't encouraged either of us to go to college, but from them we know all about our future as good wives. I've been groomed all my life for this sole ambition, and I've reached the age when it will happen. I'm looking forward to it with glee, too. Why? I can't wait to get out of my parents' house so that all the fighting and screaming will stop.

Finally, I'll have a place where I belong. With Steve's love, everything will turn out great and the craziness will finally stop!

It's a lazy weekend afternoon with Steve, and I find myself standing in my bedroom, overhearing him on the phone in the living room. Who's he talking to?

I strain to overhear. In a barely audible voice, he's apologizing. Fumbling through excuses to someone for why he hadn't shown up.

Where else was he supposed to be?

Then it hit me all at once. The gaps of silence in Steve's conversation belong to the distant voice of a woman. *Another* woman. Someone I knew nothing about.

Was he, could he be—how could he be seeing someone else? Shock thrums through my bones. The dream moves into a nightmare and the players and their parts suddenly speed up and crash into a wall. My mind explodes.

The world flickers in and out around me. One minute I'm crying uncontrollably. The next minute I'm laughing hysterically. Then crying again. I'm a live wire, wearing my emotions on my fingertips. My body moves through space without me. I'm in the living room. In my bedroom. Where am I?

Life and the physical space around me quickly become a blur. Emotions tear through me like a tornado, and I go somewhere far away to get out of the path of this storm. I'm already living outside of my body most of the time, and Steve has become my only reason to be in it. Now that's gone. *Gone.*

What I say next terrifies both Steve and my parents who are present in the house. The straw that breaks the camel's back happens in that moment. All the years of overcompensating for the stress, confusion, and craziness in and around me come falling in like dominoes. I tell them clearly, "I want to die."

That's how, at age 17, I found myself in lock-down at a psych ward: Steinberg building, fifth floor, Jewish Hospital. It has its own elevator with a special key. Once again, I can't remember the ride there or the check-in process. Everything blurs around me, like I'm looking at the world through a rain-spattered window.

How had this happened?

Three years prior, starting at age 14, I'd cycled through countless psychiatrists in New Mexico and Texas. Then our family had received a new military placement in O'Fallon, Illinois, and I embraced it as a fresh start. Dad was finally living close to the wife and children of his only brother, who had mentored him but died young. Even though my father could no longer spend time with his brother, at least he could now have all of his brother's friends nearby. Time with friends and family would help him put the painful experiences from Thailand, the war and our tumultuous experience in New Mexico behind him. We would be a family again.

My mother, too, seemed hopeful for the first time in many years. She got a job and buried herself in the details of setting up a new house, which we purchased instead of using Air Force base housing or renting—more seeming stability. For the first time, we owned a home in a neighborhood off the military base. My room was my own, not a short-term place that could be taken away at any moment. Had we found our way out of the vicious loop between alcohol and emotion that had dominated our family life these many years?

But the men my father reconnected with turned out to be his brother's old cronies... drinking buddies. As we settled in, my father began spending more and more time with them, in the same taverns and bars that his brother had frequented. My father held his time with these buddies as sacred. Along with keeping him drinking, it also kept him away from us.

Nothing was more painful to my mom, of course, who still wanted attention and affection in the worst way. Even though she had hurt my dad, I could sense she wanted their marriage to work again. But like me, she felt powerless and invisible.

The failure of this new start hit me like a punch in the gut. Coming there was supposed to make everything different. But this was just the same old crap. More than ever, I wanted—no, I needed—a place to belong. At school, I was the new girl once again, the outsider.

Luckily, I had booze. I knew I could count on alcohol to find me friends.

But as I picked up my first drink in Illinois, the old problems quickly found me. Soon enough, I was hanging out with older kids, drinking, and blacking out. On my way home from school one day, I ran into friends in the park who invited me to join them for a beer. One minute, I was having a few beers. Next, I'm calling my parents from a pay phone in Hopkinsville, Kentucky. "I don't know how I got here," I told my mother honestly. I was still holding my school bag full of books, with no idea what else had happened.

My parents were fuming. Once again, they needed to pull me out of some faraway hole. What had they done to deserve a daughter like this?

Meanwhile Ron was in high school a year ahead of me and staying busy mowing lawns, working at a restaurant, and playing baseball... and staying invisible so as not to bring the wrath of our Dad down on him also. Dad kept his physical attacks on Ron to backhand him and control him by intimidation.

At least I was getting attention from my family. Even negative attention seemed better than nothing. So I continued doing whatever I could to get it. I spent a good part of my teenage years this way, my parents gradually growing accustomed to, if not accepting of, the madness in me. I found myself coming to hate those experiences and then of course, hating me.

At school, I imagined I was being talked about behind my back. In my magical mind, I was terrorized by the madness of my behavior.

I terrorized myself even though I was treated mostly with kindness by my peers. That gap haunted me constantly—the gap between who I really wanted to be as a friend, daughter, sister, and student, and the behavior that took me out of the care I felt somewhere deep inside for them.

Thus, as the days pass in the ward, I begin having the vague sense that the relationship, the dream of a sane life with Steve would soon come to a permanent end. A few weeks later when he comes to tell me as much, I feel no surprise. But after he leaves the room, the finality of it rips me open. Once again, I've failed. Miserably.

Love, care, connection—other people can have that stuff. Me, I don't deserve any of the perks in life. How stupid I feel to believe that someone like Steve could actually love me.

Either out of kindness or pity, my mom, dad, aunt, uncle, cousin, and a few girlfriends come to visit me in the psych ward. But we don't know what to say to each other anymore. While my peers are busy buying prom gowns and sending graduation announcements, I'm doing my best to fit in with the half dozen other young people I live with in the psych ward.

My new peer group at the hospital has more radical views than any of the kids I'd encountered in high school, which opens me up for the first time to the notion that I can think for myself. We take comfort in the music of James Taylor, which pulls us younger residents from the sterile hospital rooms where we sleep into the common room where we listen together to the music of the late 60's and early 70's.

I sprawl out on the couch and together we sing, "I've seen lonely times when I could not find a friend," and then, "All you've got to do is call and I'll be there. You've got a friend." I sing along, and these songs become my anthems. I desperately need to believe James.

During times on the ward when we're allowed to socialize, I watch one man march up and down the halls, literally crowing and flapping his arm-wings like a rooster. Other residents tell me he had held a prominent position in the community making lots of money before he cracked. Is this really happening? I'd been weepy, sure. Plenty of times I'd cried myself to sleep. But this man seems truly crazy to me. Do I actually belong here?

I replay James Taylor's songs in my mind over and over as I try to understand why my family had sent me here. I'd wanted to die many times and I'd said as much... even acted on it. Why would this propel them to send me to the loony bin? At home, the fighting in my family had begun generating a certain degree of chaos. But at least we had a modicum of normalcy, too. In the morning, my parents went to work. I went to school. Ron stayed busy. At times at night, my mother would make dinner and then we watched TV together.

But I'd been yanked out of that structured life and put into a mixed-up, upside-down world with no clear boundaries or routines. I won't even get to finish my senior year of high school. I'm now orbiting another planet, one my girlfriends would never understand.

The life we had once shared, with lockers and football games and school dances, now ceases to exist for me.

I hate this place. I hate my life.

During the day, nurses give me meds. In theory, they're to keep me balanced. In reality, the meds keep me confused, wandering around in a haze of old emotions like stacks and stacks of papers that haven't been properly sorted. I still have no answers for the psychiatrist's questions that perplex me when they ask, "How do you feel? Why do you run away?" They ask me questions, and all I can think is, "I have no idea what to say to you." To me, it seems like yet another series of multiple-choice questions, but with no answer options provided. My mind is living inside of a punching bag, trying to find its way out.

At night, I get different meds, barbiturates to put me to sleep. In the midst of so much turmoil, the drugs offer my only reprieve.

Could things possibly get any worse?

The answer is, yes. Because next, an aloof doctor in a starched white coat delivers two of the most charged words in a young woman's vocabulary: "You're pregnant."

Pregnant?

I'm mortified.

Pregnant.

I'm happy.

Pregnant?!?

I'm ashamed.

I'm elated.

Emotions zigzag inside me. One minute I feel hopeful, the next terrified, and then everything in between.

Of course, when my family put me in a psych ward, they had never considered even once that something besides mental illness might have been fueling my emotional instability. Yet I'd been stewing in the hormonal chaos of pregnancy for a month now. Like many women, including my mother, the extra estrogen and progesterone my body is cranking out makes me extra sensitive, a sensitivity that my drinking has amplified. Pregnancy, not lunacy, has made me hysterical.

But the powers that be have already officially pronounced me crazy. And I see myself through their eyes.

The disjointed thoughts race through my mind one after the other. How can a crazy woman like me raise a child? On the other hand, how can I *not* raise this child, Steve's child? Besides, maybe I won't feel so alone with a baby to watch. Thinking this way for a few minutes brings me a little moment of calm, then I wonder again, what kind of future would this child have with a mom like me? Should I give the child up for adoption? Will I have the strength to do something so painful?

Sometimes I can't think straight at all. The drugs make me cloudy and numb. I keep grasping at the decision, only to find it slipping away from me.

In the end, what I want doesn't matter. Even though it's 1971 and abortion is still illegal, my doctors get special permission for me to have a therapeutic abortion. They tell me that I'm not mentally capable of carrying, or caring for, a child. Both of my Catholic parents and Steve agree. My parents schedule the abortion without asking me what I think or how I feel.

Dammit! How dare they! They have no right to block me out of this decision! Who the hell do they think they are, barging into my life this way?

I'd spent my entire childhood with a muzzle—everything was, "Yes, sir. No sir. Yes, ma'am, no ma'am," even when I wanted to scream at the top of my lungs, "Stop! You never ask me a question, listen to my ideas, or let me explore my own imagination!" I'd lived as a mannequin—stiff, perfectly clothed, standing at attention until shown what to do or how to be next.

But at 17, I'm now starting to see through all that BS. Adults around me are living in a world that has them mask their dreams and cares, and they want me to follow, marching with a thousand others. Only if *I* comply will *they* feel normal. "The emperor has no clothes!" I want to scream at them. "Take back your muzzle, and let me be and live on my terms."

Underneath all that rage, I hear a small part of me wonder if my parents and the doctors might be right. Maybe I really can't raise a child. But I shove that voice back down. I don't know and I don't care if they had made the right decision for me. They had stolen my choice. I have a good reason to be pissed, and I'll never forgive any of them for this.

The wall grows ever higher.

Under all that angry bravado, I feel terror. A good Catholic girl would never find herself in this situation. No one in my family had ever spoken about abortion, except as a grave sin against God. How would God punish me for doing something so unthinkable?

Maybe the doctors are Catholic, too, since none of them are telling me anything about what might happen before, during, or after this... this what? Is it an operation? A procedure? Or just a mortal sin? All I know for sure is that in a few hours, I won't be pregnant anymore, and an immense wave of shame washes over me.

A wispy, green elastic cap haloes my face as I wait on a gurney in a cold, empty hallway. Under a thin hospital gown, my naked skin prickles with goosebumps. I inhabit a cold, sterile world now. If I'd hated my father for the exam he'd ordered for me in New Mexico to check on the state of my virginity, that had only been a beginning. All the same feelings swirl through me now, but louder, scarier, angrier. Somehow, the pain dial on my life keeps going up.

I have no idea how long I lie there, tears streaking my face. Of course, I'm alone. And by now, I've come to expect this feeling of utter loneliness.

So I'm surprised to feel someone beside me that afternoon in the hallway outside the operating room. He's a medical assistant, young, maybe in his early 20s. Silently he reaches for my hand. As I cry, he holds it. At least for a moment, someone finds me. Sees me. This stranger's kindness makes an unexpected pillow of relief around me.

As quickly as he appears, however, he vanishes, swallowed by the echoing hallway behind me as the medical team pushes me into the operating room ahead.

Mining for Grace

Looking back, I can see that my parents' version of me as a crazy person had been building for a long time, based on a combination of their experiences with me going missing for periods of time and a general lack of knowledge around alcoholism—let alone any of this happening for such a young girl.

From the very first sip at age 12, I was what they call a blackout drinker. Neither my parents nor I, of course, knew anything about blackout drinking or what it means to be an alcoholic. It was the late 60's, and alcohol was simply a part of life, a presence at every party and wedding I attend with my family, even at every church social. No one ever talked about someone drinking too much unless they just, "have a few too many," like my mom's report of my dad when I was small. No big deal, just a few too many. As long as a person can function "normally," meaning, get to work in the morning, do their job, and keep from drinking before the evening, alcohol is a non-issue.

Now I can feel the perplexing question that must have resided in them during this time: "What is happening to my daughter?" Also, sometime in my teens, I recalled my mother making a passing mention of having had a "nervous breakdown" before I had been born. Watching me unravel this way must have terrified her, forcing her to relive that horrible experience from her past and instilling a deep fear of my life turning out like hers. Therefore, she couldn't meet my pain and suffering with love and curiosity. No way was my mother going to let my emotions get out of hand.

And no way would my dad—who didn't have any way of expressing his own tender emotions either, and had come to his wit's end trying to control me—see my rage at Steve's actions as anything other than a last straw, a psychological break.

At the time, I, too, had no way to see anything except from their perspective. I was obviously mentally ill and needed to be locked up for my own safety.

Yet through all of this insecurity, terror, blame, physical pain, and more, divine grace showed up again and again. And now after many years of reflecting upon this time in my life, I've gained this perspective: I *know* that grace shows up even more when we look for it. Partly I know this from all the years I spent looking for its opposites, things like the loneliness I felt in the hospital bed the day of my suicide attempt. I'd practiced being angry, upset, lonely. Even when drops of divine grace fell on me, I had a habit of looking at the gloomy, gray clouds, not the cleansing rain. I saw life through the lens of pain, to the point that I didn't only encounter painful experiences, I created them.

Miraculously, though, grace never abandons us completely. Even when we *don't* have our attention turned toward it, grace is constantly finding moments to bless us, the way a tango dancer and partner find that perfect moment of balance... the precise connection. Though I couldn't recognize these moments as grace-filled at the time, they were there... the moment with the young medical assistant who treated me with real kindness, or the fact that the soundtrack of my time in the psych ward was sung by James Taylor, who had himself struggled with addiction. My life has been filled with countless moments of this precise connection, this grace, even during the toughest times.

In high school, my psychology teacher, Mrs. Bosworth, whom I deeply respected, told me that I was a good person. I doubt she remembers saying it, yet at some of my worst moments, her words would unexpectedly come back to me. If this woman thought I was good, then maybe something about me could be salvaged after all.

The closer I look, the more stories of grace I can spot

lodged in the shadowy caves of my past. Because I have now trained my focus on grace, I see that life brims with untapped blessings, unknown possibilities, unrecognized miracles. I have become a collector of grace, mining my history for the things I overlooked, treasures I left behind.

Of course, I didn't have much experience with this in my early years, and it felt at that time that my life was being shaped by madness rather than grace. I did, however, have tiny little moments of hope... plenty of them. And perhaps these were little droplets of grace that were accumulating under the surface that whole time.

For example, every time my family moved, a little bit of hope would enter me—a belief that we could start over, that I could make things turn out differently. Over time, they would crash around me in the same old way so that eventually I became cynical. I told myself not to indulge in the luxury of hope anymore.

Dating Steve had me believe that someone new could save me from all the pain. Our time together changed my perspective on relating to others and some of the cynicism was temporarily washed away. All the time I spent thirsty for alcohol, I'd actually been thirsty for love. I still believed someone outside me could provide it, the same way I'd thought a new place would change the old patterns in our family. Then my relationship with him turned out to be a lot like our move to Illinois. Not a fresh, but a false, start.

Each time I experienced disappointment, I became more and more fragile, so that by the time I learned of Steve's infidelity, I broke. At such a young age, I already felt I'd used up my last chance at happiness.

I didn't yet understand that each new beginning, whether in a new place or with a new boyfriend, worked like a new train on old tracks. Even though everything looked fresh and shiny on the outside, I'd done nothing internally to lay down new tracks to truly take me in a new direction. Without new ways of thinking and seeing the world, the narrow rails of my brain patterning would carry me only in the same circle, to the same place, every single time.

When I found myself pregnant, some part of me hoped for another new beginning. Had my parents been out of line to set up an abortion for me without talking to me first? Possibly. And losing the choice about something so personal as motherhood surely would have proven painful for almost anyone in my shoes. Naturally, I felt angry.

Yet I didn't just get angry at them. I *became* the anger. Looking back now, I have to admit that the 17-year-old me couldn't have made a decent decision about whether or not to have a child. Yet my mind kept hold of rage the way a child holds onto her or his favorite toy, refusing to share. A wobbling, scratched record played over and over again inside me: Abortion, abortion, abortion, you assholes. Look what you did to me.

I would show them. I would hurt them by staying angry for life.

So I laid down another set of looping tracks that would undermine any future new beginnings I made. I let rage over this situation cripple me for many years, never admitting to myself any other version of the story. Also, because the anger was happening primarily inside, rather than outside, me, I thought only I was hurting. Now I know we were all hurting.

At the time I believed the difficult events in my life had dealt me an impossible hand. Poor me. Why even try? The victim emerged once again.

Still, something in me didn't give up entirely.

What I know now, having developed great love and compassion for myself, is that the depth of the emotional pain of these events would actually play the biggest role in determining what would come next. Just as I had unconsciously trained myself to first see the impossibility, the despair and hopelessness, I would now need to train my attention on a new way of seeing—on grace—if I ever wanted to truly change my life.

However, I'm not suggesting that letting go of the

feeling of being a martyr or victim of your life's circumstances is easy. That turning your attention toward grace is something you can simply choose to do right now and suddenly everything makes sense. What I *am* suggesting is that we often victimize ourselves after the events are long gone by repeating the same verse to an old song over and over again without really listening to what we're singing. Over time, we learn that we get to change the melody and the lyrics and embrace a new tune as we look at life, which includes both despair and grace-filled moments.

I have great compassion for our journeys and the time they take, which is different for each of us. I have a friend who calls this the "pace of grace." The nature of grace is that it's always present, and each time we integrate an experience from our past, we get a glimpse through the clouds, no matter how momentary. Eventually, we see that the accumulated drops have become a lake of nourishment that can wash us clean over and over.

Deeper Down the Rabbit Hole

*"It's no use going back to yesterday,
because I was a different person then."*

~ Alice, in Lewis Carroll's "Alice in Wonderland"

When I get out of the car in front of a stereotypical Midwestern home one July evening in 1971, I have no idea what's coming. The two-story house with a gabled roof and narrow, trim lawn looks back at me with more or less the same blank expression as all the others in this residential neighborhood by the Belleville fairgrounds. A clean front porch, with asphalt siding and a plain brown door. Everything about the place screams normal. Little do I know that my life is about to change forever.

Inside, I find the party I expect, typical in every way. Drinks wait around the corner, and the first floor is swarming with people already drunk. Some sway to the loud music, and a few dance at the center of the room. But most just stand around talking. Hot girls in short skirts, hotter guys with full, long hair. This is my scene. A place where I belong.

Only after I settle in with my own drink do I notice something different this time. A protective cluster of people has now collected at the bottom of the staircase in the home. Are they guarding something? A few members step through the group, swallowed by a pool of shadows as they climb. The mystery of it tugs at me. What's going on upstairs?

At some point, I get invited to find out. Already buzzed from the alcohol, I stumble with my friend Bob across the invisible line at the base of the staircase.

The dimly lit room where I find myself next makes a sharp contrast to the party downstairs. No music here, no loud talking, no celebration. Just six or seven people in pairs or triads, all of them focused on one thing: getting needles into their arms.

My body is singing for something to stop the jagged feelings I'm living with since leaving the hospital, and the alcohol hasn't been doing the job. I watch the face of a man nearby in an overstuffed chair. As he pushes the plunger of the syringe that hangs near the crook of his elbow, his face blossoms.

I watch in both fear and wonder. This looks like an orgasm

without the sex, maybe something even better—or maybe something worse. I watch his entire body unfold like a map to bliss.

My friend Bob asks, "Do you wanna get off?" I don't even ask what's in the syringe. I immediately say yes.

Which says a lot. As a kid, I was so afraid of needles that my mom and the nurse of the moment usually had to chase me around the room, then practically sit on top of me to give me shots. My aversion to them had never wavered, until now. I'd just gotten out of the loony bin at the Jewish hospital. I'm smothered in feelings of great loss— my boyfriend, my high school degree, my baby, and my pride, all in a matter of months. The sting of a needle seems like nothing next to these gaping wounds.

If I can come away feeling half as good as that man's face said I would, enduring a little pin prick would be worth it. The needle looks harmless. A little edgy, maybe, but I quickly tell myself that this is only a one-time thing anyway... it's a new experience and I can handle it.

The needle still makes me nervous enough, though, so I ask Bob to help me get it in. Then, the plunger goes down. In an instant, my hesitation evaporates. The pain vanishes, too. All of it. At that moment I feel safe... held. The feeling of being rocked in a mother's arms.

Liquid barbiturates pump through my veins. Everything around me becomes slow and radiant. For once, the world seems not perilous, but warm and drowsy. This... this is what I'd seen on that man's face. It feels better than any seduction, bigger than any orgasm. How fortunate that I have the courage to try things other people were too scared to do. Only someone who has tried it can understand. This dope feeling is beautiful.

No one could have convinced me that night, in that quiet, shadowed room, that I was shooting myself up with slow, ugly suicide.

Upon leaving the psych ward two months before, I'd hit the wall of the big bad world. My parents sent me looking for a job with no high school degree and no real-world experience. I hated them. I hated my life. I hated myself. I'd turned into something worse than just a failure. I was—as I'd always feared—a complete misfit.

One afternoon I found myself driving my parents' car from O'Fallon to the neighboring town of Belleville on a job lead from the paper. I saw a man walking along the roadside, thumb out. On a whim, I decided to pick him up. About 5'9" with wiry red-brown hair sticking out at odd angles, the man told me his name: "Hound Dog." It fit. His zany personality filled up the car, but in a way I really enjoyed. I felt alive around this guy. Finally, after so much time by myself, I was connecting with someone.

Hound Dog asked me to take him to a place called the American Eagle. I hadn't heard of it, but any excuse to blow off this impossible job search seemed like a good one. At Hound Dog's direction, I found my way to a small, older house with a gabled roof and a large front porch, just a block off Main Street in Belleville, IL. The place had been recently converted from a home into a store. Hound Dog invited me to join him.

As I stepped through the door, a powerful aroma, rich and sweet, hit me hard. I smelled incense for the first time. Lynyrd Skynyrd's "Free Bird" is playing in the background, with bins of records lining small rooms where people were strung about lounging and talking. I instantly liked the vibe and felt curious about the records that I found myself browsing. But more than anything else, I liked the American Eagle because Hound Dog wanted me there. I can't remember the last time someone actually wanted me.

That day became the first of many I would spend at the American Eagle. In time, I met the owners—Gary with his long, wiry, disheveled hair and big mustache, and Wayne, a dwarf. Both outsiders by appearance, these men acted more like hosts of a party than the owners of this little head shop. Theirs is a world forbidden by my father. But here, I could finally relax, open up. I sensed that my past didn't matter in this place. To my great relief, I began to make friends.

Not surprisingly, someone from this crowd of misfits had been the one to invite me to the party where I found the needle. And with the needle in my arm, I felt at home. Like the hospital barbiturates, which had been my only way to get any sleep in the psych ward, intravenous drugs became my only escape from my hopeless life. Since age 12, the world had been shrinking around me like a scene from "Alice in Wonderland." Now, it has shrunk down to one thing: the next hit.

My life is now a hunt. The next hit, the next taste, the next trip. I'm obsessed. When I don't have enough money for drugs, I shoot up alcohol to get drunk really fast. While kids I'd hung out with only months prior are now getting ready for college or marriage, I'm shooting up. I find myself breaking *all* my parents' rules, wantonly. When I look in the mirror, I no longer recognize the person looking back at me.

A blanket of secrecy falls over my life. I still live at home, at least in theory. And on the outside, I do normal things like visit relatives or go out with my parents. But I now start disappearing for a handful of weeks rather than days. As time goes on, I drop in at my parents' house only long enough to clean up and recover from the last drug binge so that I can begin the next one.

Sometimes I get a sinking hunch that something is really wrong with me. On the inside, I know I care about my family, my friends, and my life overall. I'm unable to keep that awareness for long, as the physical and emotional cravings override everything. Then a quick flash of loneliness, missing my family, and longing to be normal hits me. Confusion, shame, guilt—painful emotions momentarily overpower the longing for drugs, and I vow to myself and my parents in my prayers that I will *never use again*.

Coming off my latest binge, I head home with a plan to sort it all out. But once again, I arrive home to find my parents arguing about who knows what... Dad's drinking; my volatile, escape-artist life; or perhaps it's just their inability to know how to relate to each other. Whatever in me has been broken, I know it will never get fixed here, with these people.

"Where's Ron?" I ask. I listen that not only is my life f*cked up, but my brother's is now beginning to fall like a house of cards. Mom tells me that he's quitting college after only one year and his draft number in 1971 is 19. He's engaged to Laura, a girl who my mother adores, always asking me, "Why can't you be like Laura?" My Mom and Dad are raging because Ron's leaving college sets him up for being drafted. So he decides to enter the Army for three years instead of being drafted for two and sent off to Vietnam. I can feel another shift coming, and it ain't going to be pretty. I'm out of here.

I decide to run. Again. Besides, my new habit has opened a new world for me. The drug scene has its own lingo, one I now speak fluently. Uppers and downers, smack, junk, H, China White. If someone carries "a fit," it means they always use their own special syringe. I can talk about how to "boot" the syringe and the way blood coagulates, along with a hundred other words and phrases that come with the territory of shooting up drugs. These words now form the currency of my world. I love this edgy slang, which gives me the feeling of being a part of something elite and supremely cool. Drug jargon functions for me like secret passwords that have the power to open invisible speakeasy doors.

I replace perfectly curled hair with a shag cut and carefully pressed dresses with patch-covered jeans. The innocent girl from the pages of my parents' photo albums vanishes like a girl in a magic trick. Belonging with my drug buddies now matters more to me than having my family's approval.

My new friends say, "Hey, let's party!" but that means nothing to me. I don't care about being wild, seeking thrills. I just want oblivion. And I want to be with my people. If they're partying—whatever that means—then so am I.

I turn 18 over the winter months, and I hear some of my new friends going on and on about Mardi Gras, this amazing, 24-hour party in the streets of New Orleans.

Crazy parties? Who cares? I just want to be with my drinking and drugging friends. Yet after living in O'Fallon for the past four years, I'm dying for a change of scenery, some kind of relief from the strict rules of my father, who still attempts to control me through threats of locking me out of the house—the one safe haven I have to go back to. Because addiction and illicit drugs continue to remain mostly unknown and misunderstood in the southern Illinois culture at large, he still has no idea how serious my addiction has become.

He also knows nothing about Mardi Gras and I insist that I'll be gone only a week. In typical militaristic fashion, he notes that yes, I've been on good behavior lately (or so he thinks, haha!). I lie about who's taking me and what we'll be doing, giving him a good story, and surprisingly, he eventually relents and buys it. I'm going to Mardi Gras!

A few days later, I find myself in an old, refurbished bread truck with two of my guy friends, heading south on I-55 bound for New Orleans. I hadn't asked a single question about the trip before we left—the address of where we would stay, whom we would meet when we got there, what I might need to know to take care of myself—none of it matters.

Instead of talking about all the boring stuff, we spend the drive time taking uppers, downers, and everything in between. I weigh all of 85 pounds, small enough to lie across the front dashboard of the large truck as my friend drives. I ride there for hours, basking in the sun as the road underneath us hums through my body. A new adventure lies ahead.

Then we hit New Orleans. Time to find more drugs. Before we even make it to the apartment where we're staying, we meet up with friends from Belleville in a park. Someone pulls out a bottle of wine and passes it around, and each person adds their own drug of choice without telling us what it is. "Electric wine," our ring leader says, shaking up the bottle, which we pass around again. This time, each of us drinks from it, the thrill of the unknown pulsing through our veins.

We push our way through throngs of people to a large Ferris wheel, one I can scarcely describe since I'd begun to feel high way back in the park with the first sip of this strange concoction. We all get on, then I get off—meaning, the drugs start to take hold of me in earnest as the wheel makes its loops. When the ride finishes, my friends turn right, but I turn left. I unwittingly split from the group. I have no phone number, no address, not even the name of a person or a place where our group is staying that night. I'm high out of my gourd and wandering around alone in the madness of Mardi Gras.

Luckily—providentially—some hippies from Florida take me in. This group, all peace, love, and go-with-the-flow, don't drink or drug nearly as much as my crowd. I'm so high and confused that one of their members—a muscled Native American man with long, dark hair; high cheekbones; and amber skin—ties one end of a rope to the belt loop of my jeans, and the other end to his own belt loop. That way I can't wander off alone again. I blindly follow this man and his group as I'm too high to do anything else.

Five whole days later, without a single memory of this time, I finally bump into someone from my Illinois group. He gives me the address of our place, an apartment that belongs to a man from a neighboring town to O'Fallon who's down there opening a bar in New Orleans.

Once there, I step into a small room with too many people in it, most of them high as kites. I notice some of the spaghetti that one guy was making in the small kitchen is stuck to the wall. A man on psychedelics points to the noodles, going on about huge worms.

After my disappearance, the group had nicknamed me "Fried Brain." Even in this crowd of committed drug users, I stand out as someone who has used way too many drugs. I don't seem to have a "stop" or even a "pause" button.

I'm sort of in my life, but I'm floating, tethered only loosely to my body the way I'd been to my Native American friend.

Our group finally begins the journey home almost an entire month after we had left—three weeks later than I'd promised my father, who has no phone number or address for me. My parents don't know if I'm alive or dead, and frankly, I don't care. If I thought of my father at all, I do so with righteous indignation. It serves him right for being such a hard-ass all my life!

As we make our way back up I-55, the halo of excitement that had surrounded our trip down fizzles into a haze of ache. Inside, my veins are thrumming addiction's theme song: MORE, MORE, MORE. All I want to do is to keep on slamming it. If I stop, I feel sick. Even worse, I now have to face everything I'd just done.

Back from Mardi Gras, I don't go home but call to check in and thankfully get the answering machine, telling them I'm fine and not to worry. My "friends" and I are so far from having any kind of control over our lives. A lot of the people I partied with that month ended up dead because of drugs, and I'm playing my own games of Russian roulette with death, too. I have plenty of near misses that summer. At a music festival in Indiana, I take drugs cut with strychnine that almost kill me. Luckily, someone helps me get to a hospital in time for the doctors to pump my stomach.

Later that year, I overdose from shooting up Preludin (speed) with a guy and a girl who drop me off at Christian Welfare Hospital in East St. Louis, left for dead. When my mother comes for me, the hospital staff advises her to put me in the Gateway Rehab Program. Alone with her in the hospital room, I get down on my knees, my hands laced together like I'm praying and I beg her not to do it. Gateway is known in the 1970's for shaving heads to reduce one's ego, a small concession considering the terror I have of withdrawing from drugs. With all my heart, I promise her once and for all: I will *never use again*.

When we get home, I tell her I'm leaving for a short walk to the grocery store. Neither of my parents sees me again for months.

I find myself shooting goofballs, a mixture of speed and heroin, at the suburban home of someone's parents. When my heart stops, a crowd gathers around me to get it started again. They don't call an ambulance since this will get them in trouble. Would they let me die first?

And these are the people I call friends. Ironic, considering I'd gotten involved with drugs to escape feelings of loneliness. My favorite drugs—opiates like heroin, morphine, and Dilaudid®—all act on the central nervous system to relieve pain. The pain of being an outsider has me willing to try anything. Now I trade overdose stories with other druggies the way veterans trade war stories. Finally—finally!—I have clout. I fit somewhere.

But is nowhere somewhere? None of us belong to, or with, each other. We can't. If it comes to it, I might leave someone for dead, too, just like others had done to me. Like someone stuck in a relationship with the most controlling lover imaginable, we all belong only—exclusively—to the drugs.

And that belonging costs me. My heartless paramour demands nothing short of everything. I give my body to men who can supply me with drugs, men I call my boyfriend who I'm actually leaning on for my supply. I don't care about them, at least not when I'm looking for the next high. And I'm sure that, beyond my body, they don't know how to care about me. Usually, the only thing we have in common is the one thing we both care about, the next fix.

I steal for a hit—money from my mother's purse, my father's wallet. One day I steal all of my mother's jewelry, including family heirlooms, and sell it all for one bag of heroin in East St. Louis.

I lie for a fix. By now, this comes so easily that I don't remember where the truth ends and the lies begin.

I use other people to get my drugs. To me, they are more like things than people. No one and nothing around me feels real. All that exists in the world are me and my precious, precious drugs.

After each high, however, the feeling that I've made a serious mistake washes over me for a brief moment. I think of my actions and wince. Even worse, I begin understanding that the actual experience of using, the experience of the high itself, never measures up to my anticipation of it and what it might bring me. But then the liquid "medicine" in the syringe speaks to me all over again. "I can take you away..." it says.

And sometimes it does. Heroin, the good stuff, carries me into euphoria. My nose itches, or I vomit. We call it "getting well." Then I start nodding, a sleep state where I feel myself rocked in the arms of an all-encompassing, all-forgiving mother. *Everything is okay*, I think, *everything is all okay.*

When I come to, this mother has disappeared. In her place, I have only a deeper well of pain, a nightmare. I live in this state for the next 18 months of my life...

Lesson & Blessing

#5

Matter over Mind

From the outside, that suburban house hadn't looked anything like a dope den. I now know that most of them don't. I didn't know that the best thing about shooting dope would be this one moment, the first time the needle sank into my arm.

Many years after I got sober, I would look back at the period of intravenous drug use that had nearly devoured me and wonder how my life had taken this turn. How had the daughter of a military man in suburban Illinois, who was raised to be kind and sensitive, found her way to hard-core drugs? Even with my partying friends in high school, I'd never encountered anything stronger than pot or mescaline, neither of which I cared much about. And in the early 1970's in the Midwest, drugs like heroin were only beginning to enter the mainstream. Most adults had barely even heard of intravenous drugs, and few in my world were doing them. They were more prevalent in the world of rock and roll, not in quaint Midwestern neighborhoods.

But then, I wasn't like other kids. My time in the psych ward had changed me, and I don't mean just on an emotional level. Not until I got into my 50's would I realize: Every single night for four months at age 17, nurses in white hats and tidy starched dresses had given me the barbiturate Seconal to put me to sleep, which was a common way that they dealt with psych patients' unsettled emotions at the time. How could I have known that I was becoming addicted to barbiturates? I had faithfully followed the doctors' orders.

To complicate matters, the doctors had done nothing to wean my body off of the barbiturates they had given me nightly. For months after leaving the hospital ward, my body had been buzzing with the memory of Seconal, making me restless and uncomfortable, no matter what I did. Sleep had been fitful and irregular, and I had nothing to take the edge off the torturous thoughts that followed me around like a faithful dog. Alcohol had been the relief that I reached for in the interim until I found drugs that fateful night.

You know how they always say "mind over matter," well addiction points to the fact that our bodies, our "matter," actually begin to control our minds, such that we literally cannot seem to make a different choice.

I'd never intended to become a drug addict or shoot drugs to hurt myself or anyone else. First, I wanted the emotional pain to stop. My mind had been out after me my whole life. I wanted to fit in. I longed to belong. We're all looking for belonging—whether in high school with the jocks, geeks, or whatever group you find yourself drawn to as a young person. I look back and realize that my critical thinking wasn't even yet developed inside of me. I was making decisions based on my emotions and reactions, not critical thinking. Yet little did I know that having had a predisposition to alcoholism could also lead to a predisposition to using drugs.

I thought I was going to a party to drink. I didn't intend to shoot dope. I had no reference point to ask myself: "What would this mean for my future?" And it's interesting that my first introduction to drugs was barbiturates, the very same substance I'd been given legally just a couple months before.

I had no understanding that I would lose control by using drugs, and that they are dangerous chemicals that have reactions on the body chemistry that the mind cannot control. Intravenous drug use creates an immediate rush in the body, which doesn't last long—maybe 30 seconds, a minute, maybe 3 at the most. However, as an addict, we chase the intensity of that high from the drug the entire time. But now I know it wasn't just "me" looking to quiet the mind, but the body, addicted, is now also asking to be quieted. The body and the mind are working both against and with each other at the same time.

To look at this a bit more deeply, there's the me—the mind and psyche—that doesn't want to feel all the emotions—the confusion, the disappointment in myself and my family... I want to get away. But as a teenager, I don't understand the psychological pull toward using drugs, and then I create a *second* monster—my body—which is now craving the drug, no matter how much the rational mind wants to stop using. I kept promising I would stop, but this war between the two had already begun. Then I entered the cycle of thinking I'm inherently bad and cannot be fixed, and the psyche got more compromised.

In short, my body chemistry became louder than my rational mind. It's like a merry-go-round that never stops. The mind wants to kill the pain, and the body craves the rush.

In addition, addiction freezes emotional development, and I'd been using alcohol to leave my world behind since age 12. Even though my body had matured on the outside, on the inside I was still just a 12-year-old girl. I had no sense of the consequences of my actions, no critical thinking or problem-solving skills. The way a child gets into a car with her parents, I would hop in with a gang of users without even wondering what would come next.

In the groundbreaking book on trauma called "The Body Keeps the Score," Bessel van der Kolk writes about his job in a mental institution of the 1960's when tackling and physically forcing patients to do things factored into his regular duties. When doctors convened for their weekly discussion of patients, their conversation hovered exclusively around meds, restraints, and behaviors to control. Only van der Kolk, who worked as an activities director in the evenings and weekends, ever heard the life stories of these people. At night when they couldn't sleep, patients came to him to confess the horrors of their past. Unlike the doctors, he began making a connection between those painful past events and the mental instability that they now experienced. But it would take many years for him to understand what he saw, since none of his role models yet looked at mental illness through the lens of the patients as people with real histories, struggles, and trauma... no one at that time addressed our humanity.

The ward where van der Kolk worked sounds a lot like the one I'd endured at age 17 during pregnancy. Instead of helping me heal a painful past, that mental hospital stripped away my innocence and any shred of normalcy or dignity still left in me. It even set the stage for future drug abuse.

To be perfectly honest with you, even these many decades later, revisiting my time as a hard-core drug addict can still elicit a subtle emotional response inside of me— agitation, the desire to turn away, edginess. My body somatically remembers the depths of these experiences.

And another part of me still clearly remembers the feeling of shame, guilt, surprise, or hurt over the choices I made. Addiction hurt me and those around me in so many ways. Yet I know that I must share these experiences. Not least of all, exploring these stories again has helped me to understand them better myself. By putting them into words, and on paper, I'm making peace with these shards of broken glass that are fragments of my past at a whole new level—at the level of considering them not only opportunities to learn a lesson, but as true blessings. And over time, they are becoming as beautiful as a mosaic.

"But how can you possibly consider intravenous drug use a blessing?" you might be asking. Though this period is the most difficult part of my life to truly perceive as a blessing, I now realize that if I left any part of it out I wouldn't be here with you sharing right now. Everything that happened was necessary. The first blessing is that I made it through this dark period and I'm alive and living my best spiritual life. I have an amazing life. And the other is that I'm able to share with you today my experience of the body-mind addiction cycle, to bring greater understanding to you and your loved ones.

The healing doesn't stop there. When I look back, I can see: Yes, I was a drug addict and an alcoholic. *And* I was so much more than that. I was a confused young woman trying desperately to make sense of the world. I was lost. I was definitely lonely. But I wasn't vindictive. Of course I did not set out to bring pain and suffering to other people's lives. My mind was looking for a way to feel sane, a way to feel any shred of hope in my life. My body was simply looking for a way to feel normal.

So I speak now as one voice for drug- and alcohol-addicted people. I speak for the sake of those who love them, a voice for parents and family members, in hopes I can help them understand.

If you love someone who's an addict, I know that my own stories can't erase the pain that addiction has caused. I only hope to help you understand from one point of view. What an addict does has more to do with his or her own internal experience of life and body chemistry than it does with you.

Still Struggling

"Where there is no struggle, there is no strength."
~ Oprah Winfrey

"**D**ad, I need help."

A small voice squeezes out these words, a voice like someone else's. Speaking them takes all my strength.

He stands in the doorway of my bedroom, the concern on his face is obvious. He can still see that there's some goodness in me, but my confusion and inability to trust in life, let alone the state my body is in, stands between the two of us.

It's been a little more than a month since I've returned home from the hospital after that fated suicide attempt where I was offered a choice. Had I been delusional hearing voices telling me life could get better? So far, nothing looked any better to me.

I haven't shot up any drugs since leaving the hospital. If my mind isn't so fogged over, I could appreciate the miracle in this. After all, I've been mainlining since age 17... close to 3 years now. In all that time, I'd never resisted it, not once.

But this doesn't seem like much to celebrate. I'm 19 going on 20 and I live at home again, recovering from the crippling pneumonia that had kept me in the hospital long after I had re-joined my body in the operating room. I weigh 85 pounds, and I rarely speak to anyone about the violent storm in my brain. Lying in the middle of my double bed, vibrating, crawling out of my skin, I find myself in the middle of a typical teenage setting... a pink princess phone, taffeta bedspread with purple flowers, and ruffled bed skirt. Yet I'm holding tightly onto the bed posts, bracing myself for a life I know I want, but don't know how to get.

My life resembles beach-front property after a serious hurricane. Only now I don't have the needle to help me ignore the wreckage.

So I find myself drinking whiskey and popping Quaaludes®, which eases the withdrawal. In my own mind, at least I'm not shooting up. But I can't fool myself into thinking that everything has turned out okay. Something in me knows I'm still in over my head.

When I ask for help this time, my dad listens.

In answer to my plea for help, my father sends me back into a psych facility.

It's 1973, and hard drugs are continuing to come back from Vietnam with the men who had been medicated by the military because of their war wounds, and those who learned to cope by using illegal drugs, a legacy of my father's world. Yet he still sees my behavior not as a sign of addiction but as one of mental imbalances.

I'm certainly giving him plenty of evidence to prove this theory, since the drugs I'm still on send me up and down an emotional roller-coaster that makes me look crazy to other people. You can't put sugar in a gas tank and expect your car to run. Little do I realize that's exactly what I'm doing by putting drugs and alcohol in my body, expecting myself to be able to function normally.

Also, I'm living in a time when the word "alcoholic" refers only to a drunk in the gutter. Someone like me—a supposed good girl from a good Catholic family—can't possibly be an alcoholic or an addict.

So to my father, the psych facility seems like the only place for me—a suicidal young woman with a life full of spectres.

I dread the thought of going back into a place like that—a place where I'm treated as if I'm crazy like all the other wackos in there. I already know that my family thinks I'm crazy, and over time it's become my self-identity as well.

But now I'm desperate. My dad's solution seems to me like the only one. So at 19, I willingly entered another mental facility.

Fortunately, my father checked me in this time to David P. Wohl, Sr. Mental Health Institute connected to St. Louis University Hospital. This place offers an alternative to the asylums of the time, which lock patients away from the world.

Instead, a famous architect, Gyo Obata, had designed its buildings with open courtyards, greenery, and fresh air. Departing radically from the norms of its time, the doors of this institution stay unlocked except late at night, and even then patients can leave with permission. No one here has been "committed" against his or her own will, and the average stay is about three weeks. Of course, I'm not average.

One evening, I'm sitting on the little single bed in my room, my knees tucked against my chest. As I face backwards, looking at the wall, I hear a voice inside me say, *"Who's looking out these eyes? Who's the one that's looking?"*

Where had that thought come from? Whose voice is saying these words inside my head? It feels like something bigger than me, a *Presence*? I can't explain.

Shortly after this encounter a priest walks in. His kind, warm demeanor puts me at ease. I sense his presence more than any details of his physical appearance. But before he leaves, he gives me a poster. On it, abstract shapes in vivid orange, yellow, and orange-red swirl around a simple flower. It reads, "I'm so glad you're here. It helps me realize how beautiful my world is."

Something about the poster touches me more deeply than I can comprehend. I begin to cry. For the first time since I began using, I feel like someone sees me as more than a drug addict. In this man's eyes, I'm a person. For a moment, his vision uplifts my own. I feel there may be possibilities ahead.

Days are spent in group therapy, individual therapy, and doing the Thorazine® shuffle. My mind is numb, on vacation from my real world as the insulation from "Hotel Wohl" holds me.

Shortly before Thanksgiving in 1973, Mom shows up for a visit and asks that I come out into the lounge area. I look out my door and I immediately sense something is off. There sits Jim, my brother Ron's former fiance's father. "What's he doing here?!" my mind shouts.

As I enter the visiting lounge and sit down with them, Mom begins to share she's in love with Jim and will be separating from my father. Now, how in the hell did *this* happen? Another affair from her?

The day comes for me to go home for a visit for Thanksgiving, and my stomach is twisted in knots knowing that Dad has been told Mom is leaving. So many emotions somersault in my gut. On top of everything else, the illusionary perfect American family has imploded.

The house is somber and the tidy brick ranch feels oppressive. Come Christmas, still in the psych facility, I get another pass to leave for the holiday. As I see Dad open a gift of pots and pans from Mom, I feel the confusion of our life ravaging me.

"Take me back, take me back to the Wohl!" I scream at them. I don't know how to handle all the emotions showing up for me.

And when they do take me back, I don't encounter life-changing treatment, though the mental institution does somehow offer me support in yet another moment of crisis.

I begin wrestling with a growing split within myself. For years, the good girl inside me had been warring with the wild addict. Now the good girl is trying to win. But even the good girl isn't truly "me," more like the voice of the church and my parents combined with my own vague sense of what seems right or wrong. Still, who's "me?" So many times during the course of addiction, I'd found myself pulled by a voice saying, "Hold on." But hold on to what? I have no idea why I'm even here on Earth or what life is all about. I have no idea who's the one looking through these eyes. I'm searching for answers, but no one has any that make sense to me.

After my four months at Hotel Wohl, I begin the arduous task of coming back to "normal" life. My time on the other side of the veil when I'd nearly died on the operating table had really done something to me, like a switch turned on. Things could never be the same. I go back to school, study and obtain my G.E.D., and give my certificate to my mother on Mother's Day. Finally, a high school graduate! Then I enroll in college courses and get a job at the efficiency store on Scott Air Force Base and find my first real roommate, Gambi. I shoot up heroin one more time and realize it's not worth the costs on many levels.

For the first time in my life, I'm holding down a job, and because Gambi is traveling a lot for work, I decide to get an apartment with my friend Deb whom I'd met at Belleville Area College.

I'm still partying, drinking alcohol, and using illegal drugs, but I'm no longer shooting up. I appear more functional. Seemingly miraculously, I continue staying away from heroin and other opioid drugs. My life starts to look more normal... on the outside anyway. I'm learning to play the game.

But I still lug around the shame of everything I'd done when I was using. And I still really like to party. I might be making honest money and taking better care of myself, but emotionally, I'm a little girl on the inside with little capacity to truly function as an adult.

At 21, I enter a psych facility again, for the third time. Life still feels crazy to me, and I grasp at whatever I can to make it through the madness. While at the hospital, I meet Dr. Robert Anderson, yet another psychiatrist who sits in a big leather chair behind an imposing desk.

I hear him say, "I think you are an alcoholic."

But wait. "Alcoholic" means a man, not a woman. Besides, I don't drink every day. I can't make any sense of his statement. And I haven't even told him that I drink, anyway. How could he even know?

I continue seeing this psychiatrist for a while after I leave the hospital. Appointments with him help during moments of crisis. But his label for me—"alcoholic"—never really lands. And how can I ever tell my parents I'm an alcoholic? If I'm an alcoholic, then what are they? The only person I ever thought was an alcoholic was my father, who drinks every evening and binges when he can. Strangely enough, being in a mental institution seems less of a big deal to me than this new diagnosis, since I'd become accustomed to the label of being the crazy one in the family.

Even if I embrace the idea of my real problem being alcohol (which does have some resonance even though I have so much resistance to it), I have no clue what to do about it. The psychiatrist has offered a label, but that's it. No next steps. No road to recovery. Just a word.

So onward and upward. *Pull yourself together, Linda,* I cajole. I try my best to slow down my drinking. I get a job as the assistant manager at the local Pizza Hut and go back to the task of surviving the daily grind.

Lesson & Blessing
#6

The Long Haul

For all of the insanity and dysfunction that the lineage of alcoholism had in our family and ancestors, we never abandoned one another. Dad showed up that day in my doorway, despite all the hurt and distrust we had endured over the years. My parents still brought me to hospitals, doing the best they could to find me the help they thought I needed to cure my "mental illness."

The field of psychology in the 1970's lagged far behind

today's standards. American culture stood at the forefront of the consciousness movement in the West that would blossom in later years. And my doctors were straight-laced psychiatrists, trained in dispensing meds, not in counseling clients. On top of that, I lived in the Midwest. People on the East and West Coasts might be doing yoga and reading Ram Dass, but in Illinois, no self-respecting bookstore yet had a self-help section. Most people went to church like good Christians and left therapy for the loonies and all that "out there" consciousness talk for the commie hippies.

Of course, plenty of people, my dad included, were actually addicted to alcohol. Plenty more used harder stuff, too. Housewives taking prescription drugs often had the sanction of their doctors for "mommy's little helper." But all this was happening long before movements like M.A.D. or the war against drugs. Very few people had the language to describe the experience of addiction. Because we couldn't speak openly about it, addiction haunted many of us like a ghost.

I've learned a lot about the way dopamine receptors in the brain play into the process of becoming addicted. The downregulation of dopamine receptors, which makes the higher highs and lower lows, makes it extremely hard for many to come off of addictive substances. Luckily, the dopamine receptors in the nucleus accumbens start repairing themselves the minute you stop using.[5]

But even when you quit a substance, whether alcohol, drugs, cigarettes, or even sugar, you still face a process of brain rehabilitation that goes beyond dopamine receptors.

Why? When you were using, the part of the brain called the hippocampus was laying down memories of the rapid sense of satisfaction you get from the substance you used. Find yourself facing a stressful day? Suddenly your brain remembers, whether or not you want it to, how great it felt to use the substance of choice to get yourself out of that stressful feeling.

This is why users can go for long periods of time without taking the substance, only to suddenly relapse. The dopamine circuits have become dormant in the brain, but the memory of the fix remains. When a user hits a life challenge—whether large or small—it can have the effect of activating a desire to want to feel normal, and "normal" is when I'm on alcohol or drugs. For me, even going to a grocery store, having to make seemingly simple purchase decisions, was enough to create the stress that would turn those circuits back on.

Your brain also lays down neural pathways during addiction that connect moods, situations, and places with the feeling the substance gave you. Something as simple as

[5] See Appendix B

reconnecting with an old friend from the drugging scene can signal the brain's memory of that fast high, and with it, difficult cravings.

This aspect of the brain's wiring also explains why a deeper level of healing, one that goes beyond just mending the dopamine receptors in the brain by getting off of the substance, plays such an important role in recovering from addiction. Addictive behaviors stem from an attempt to escape or deny painful feelings from the past. Heavy emotions that we experience, difficult situations we don't know how to face—these all affect long-term recovery. As long as these underlying motivations for substance abuse remain in place, we risk reverting back to the old habit of using.

So for me, just as the *Presence* had promised from the other side, there were small signs that my life *was* getting better. However, as someone newly introduced to the idea that another issue might be alcoholism rather than only drug addiction and mental illness, it felt like the slow train to nowhere. I don't know exactly what I'd expected, but this molasses-moving improvement was not it.

At that time, I was coping with life in the mind-scape of addiction, a realm where the pain was still so great that my tendency was to give up right before the miracle—I didn't yet trust the process. I believed I'd found a true sense of belonging in hard drugs and the community of users. Only after stopping shooting up could I see that these drugs and friends had never really been on my side—that I'd been alone in addiction all along. Even as I had this realization and found some brief reprieve, new layers of unworthiness were revealed to me as the next diagnosis of "alcoholic" came out. This then brought more confusion that required even bigger miracles to tell me to keep turning toward, rather than away from, my problems. That's what the priest and poster represented— another experience of *Presence* revealing itself to me in the form of a person rather than the light that had engulfed and spoken to me in the hospital.

The poster indicated to me that there might be a reason that I'm in the world, more than I could imagine. There was care and generosity in the priest that made me feel that I mattered. This was a first glimpse at something I would be able to see more and more... *I'm so glad you're here. It helps me realize how beautiful my world is.*

I had no healthy concept of God in those days. I suppose I expected the journey after being told life would get better to be a lot easier than it had been. I thought something would happen to me, from the outside, receiving the roadmap to life. Had I really signed up for this grueling, uphill climb? I was working a menial job, seeing a psychiatrist, even finding myself back in a mental institution more than once. On the outside, my life didn't look miraculously changed.

Even if I couldn't see it then, I was developing stamina by showing up every day in my life. When things got hard enough to trip the brain wires of craving buried in my memory—oh, the ache for dope!—I still kept myself away from the needle. Quietly, arduously, I was building the muscles to lift myself into the miracle I'd been offered by being in the hospital, the promise of a better life.

I didn't know yet that the real miracle, the one I'd yearned for, was one that could happen only on the inside. Not through something I did or got, but from the woman I became. A woman who could both hear and begin to be led by deeper questions that were beginning to penetrate me: *Who is looking through these eyes? Who am I, why am I here, and what is life really all about?*

These awakening moments began to break up the story that I'd carried about myself for so long. They poked holes in the certainty about who I held myself to be—the problem, crazy, unlovable, unworthy, I don't belong. At first glance, this awareness may not seem like much. You can't put it in the bank or use it to feed a family. And yet it continued to feed and nourish me, and planted seeds for the future growth I would experience.

Under all the drinking and drugs, under the feverish scramble to belong, this was brewing under the surface and finally had space to come out in an unexpected place—a psych ward with a priest and a psychiatrist!

We have no idea what a miracle looks like because we often don't get to see the outcome until much later. Instead, we give our attention to our judgments, our disappointments, shame, and feelings, that often stem from our cultural, religious, and family upbringing. Like my twisted yet perfect journey, it may require you or your loved ones to go into a psych ward, give up friendships, and question everything. I encourage you to open to deeper acceptance of the pace of life's journey, even when it doesn't look like you're headed in the right direction.

The Miracle of Hitting Rock Bottom

"Rock bottom became the solid foundation
on which I rebuilt my life."
~J.K. Rowling

Outside, the Illinois summer air is weighted down with wet heat, the kind that makes the simple act of breathing an unpleasant task. No way am I leaving my little efficiency apartment that Sunday morning to brave it. The summer of 1979 finds me in this sparse little place, less a home than a crash pad. I use it for brief rest stops between the blurred bursts of chaos that I know as my life.

It's now been four years without shooting up heroin,

barbiturates, or any other drugs, but I still use drugs like cocaine and pharmaceuticals, as well as alcohol, every single day. And my intake is progressing. Instead of drinking only in the evenings, I now take Valium® in the morning because I don't want to drink before work— only alcoholics do that and I'm still not embracing that diagnosis. I've been working in a pharmacy as the bookkeeper since 1977. It might as well be a candy store. Deb has long since moved away, intolerant of my erratic behavior and victim mentality, leaving me alone once again.

Sunday mornings catch up with me week after week. My still completely addicted body uses drugs Monday through Saturday simply to stay alive, but I drink every day and am sent into oblivion, easily able to forget the pain of my past. I tell myself I need to clean up because there's a new week ahead. The itch is constant.

I'd grown up seeing Sundays as family day. As much as I might deny it, I yearn for the family I never had, one where I feel I belong. Finding myself in a tiny, empty apartment on a day like this only underscores how impossible this dream has become.

On this Sunday, like so many before, I'm lying on the couch, unable to do much more. My head hurts. My body aches. But the loudest pain I feel leaks out from a broken heart. Misery and self-loathing have cornered and pummeled me once again.

Then something happens. Without my bidding, a plea rises up in my throat from somewhere deep.

"God!" I cry. I say it out loud, calling out like a girl who looks in a crowded room for her lost father. I hit bottom. I know I can't keep on living this way. But I have no idea how to make a change, either. Everything I'd tried so far had failed.

"God! I can't stand the pain anymore. Please help me!" I yell out loud. And I say the prayer I have said plenty of times: "God get me out of this mess, and I'll *never* do it again!" But something about this one—my sincerity, or the despair from which I'm calling out... something about this prayer feels different. I not only gave up, I also gave in, admitting to myself and to God that I can't get out of this mess on my own. I *surrender*.

And my prayer lands. I speak and something happens, something invisible but still tangible to me. This is an experience I'd searched for when attending Christian church and was saved—transactional analysis, confession, switching drinks, switching drugs, etc., all for the purpose of finding an answer.

This moment with God gets me through that Sunday with a little more grace than usual. As I get ready for work the next morning, I notice I'm breathing a little easier.

Then I head back to the daily grind of work, co-mingled with addiction. That moment on the couch doesn't take long to recede into the background.

Little do I know, however, that something actually had happened that summer Sunday. Along with the lessons, the blessings of my life would soon become real to me for the first time.

About two weeks after my forgotten Sunday encounter with God, I find myself in a much more familiar experience: clutching a drink at The Double Eagle bar in O'Fallon, Illinois. Though I have been consciously avoiding going to the same bar too often so that no one suspects how much I need alcohol, I do drink somewhere every single night. Usually I meet up with friends, and the pattern is that I almost always black out before the evening is over. I don't care. I never even considered life without my dear friend liquor.

The neighborhood's younger crowd frequents The Double Eagle, a corner hangout with large, street-front windows and the rustic, old-time atmosphere of a saloon.

Fred had purchased the place a few years before as a sideline income for himself and his fiancé, who tended the bar while he worked his other job. But when Fred, drunk, had rolled his truck on the night of his own bachelor party, everything had changed. The accident had left him a paraplegic. With this, both his job and his fiancé disappeared. But that didn't stop Fred from living. As soon as he could, he began working behind the bar, which became his sole income. In time, he bought a boat, which he took me out on. His positive attitude had inspired respect in many of his regulars, including me. Any trip to The Double Eagle meant a chance to see Fred.

But when I step into the bar that evening, Jerry is one of the first people I see. Jerry and I had attended high school together. Now he works with my father, who had been doing Union day labor since he had retired from the military.

At the bar, I order my usual—whiskey and water.

Jerry says offhandedly, "Oh, you drink just like your dad."

When my throat burns with the next sip, the liquor isn't to blame. Jerry might as well have shoved his fist in my stomach. Never mind the fact that this place stands on the same corner as my father's favorite bar just a few streets down, where he's probably sitting drinking at this very moment. So what if I order the same drink he did or held the glass in my hand the same way? I'm nothing like that old bastard. Somewhere below the surface, I blame my dad's drinking for causing many of our family's problems, and Jerry's words twist the old knife in even deeper.

I down another then another, drinking myself as quickly as I can, away from the dark, wood-paneled room, away from the pool tables, darts and shiny bar in front of me, away from Jerry and my dad and everything else. Getting to a safe place comes as easily as another drink. The blackout? I don't have to feel this pain.

Four hours later, I begin to emerge from that blackout state. Somewhere along the way, Fred had taken my keys, and now I want them back. But he refuses. Instead, he gets someone to collect me from the barstool like one more thing to clean up at the end of the night. Against my protests, they deposit me in his little apartment upstairs.

When I finally wake the next morning, I watch Fred pull himself out of bed, limb by limb. Just this simple act, something I do every day without thinking, seems like a feat of stamina and courage for him. Witnessing it leaves me in awe. To me, a life like his, with only half a functioning body, seems like a waking nightmare. Yet Fred doesn't live his life like he's half a man. He's strong, determined. Never once did I see him feeling sorry for himself.

"You know," Fred begins that morning, "I used to think you brought class when you came into the bar, and when you left you took it with you."

I know what he's implying. I work hard at looking good. No matter how tangled up I feel on the inside, I make sure to put myself together for the outside world. But Fred isn't finished talking.

"It turns out, you're a drunk just like the rest of them. Get your ass out of bed, Linda, and get to work. And stop using people."

Fred's words sink into me like a dart in the center of the board. If anyone can speak to me this way, it's Fred. He's earned the right with his own example.

Speechless, I gather myself up from Fred's little place and head into work wearing yesterday's wrinkled clothes. On the inside, I feel even more crumpled, like an empty milk carton crushed under a tire. Fred's words still echo through my mind.

In a stroke of good fortune, I'd scored my job at the pharmacy by flirting shamelessly with Craig, a young man I met at a wedding three years prior who had been studying to become a pharmacist.

"I used to be a drug addict," I'd told him over drinks in a confidential tone. I'd never mentioned all the alcohol or the pills I still use. In my mind, I truly believed I wasn't addicted anymore if I wasn't shooting up. And I knew I didn't want to be that person—the junkie—anymore. Of course, working around drugs all day sounded great, a lucky break. Goodbye pizza pie, hello Percocet®.

That morning, though, I leave Fred's feeling anything but lucky. Defensively, I arrive late to work. Why does it matter if I show up on time or not, as long as I put in my eight hours? Eventually, I would fully understand Fred's advice to stop taking advantage of other people—even if I knew deep down the moment he had said it that he had nailed me.

I begin each workday by knocking back a Valium® or Percocet®, whatever I can pocket. Somewhere along the way, I'd picked up an unspoken social message that drinking in the day signaled a problem with alcohol. These pills become my next best solution. Taking pharmaceuticals seems like a lesser evil than daytime booze. I use my well-honed cunning skills to get my hands on drugs every day. I figured out that I can distract the pharmacists if I turn up with donuts and make coffee, so I quickly make this my daily routine. I burn into my brain the pathways through the maze of inventory to every drug I like, so that during the handful of minutes when my colleagues step away from the counter to get a donut and have a coffee break, I have just enough time to grab a treat of my own. This gets me through my morning.

But today, I show up late, with no goodies in hand. By now, customers are gathering, and I'd missed the window when the pharmacists would leave their posts. I can't nab even a single pill.

Soon, my whole body starts shaking. I have no idea how I'll make it through this day. Even though I'd logged my time in psych wards and psychiatrist offices, I still have no real concept of what a liar and addict I am. Alcohol and drugs are simply a way of life. I do, however, have Fred's speech echoing through my head. Any other day, I might have white-knuckled it until I could come up with a new strategy for stealing drugs to maintain or stop the shakes. Today, I can't shake the sense that I've been heading down the wrong road for far too long. It's been 13 years since my first sip of alcohol.

As indiscreetly as possible, I snag the heavy phone book from the counter and lug it into a corner. Licking my fingers, I begin thumbing through the thin pages for the number to ADCO, a drug and meth-adone clinic I'd attended years before. With no other way to stop the shakes, I became intent on reaching the counselor who had won my confidence. I huddle over the phone receiver and dial.

I don't understand exactly what happens next. Surely I'd dialed ADCO. Yet the woman who answers has nothing to do with ADCO.

"This is Alcoholics Anonymous. How can I help you?" the woman states.

Alcoholics Anonymous? What is she talking about? I look down at the page, my finger still planted next to the ADCO number. Had I misread it? I'd never heard of Alcoholics Anonymous, but for some reason, I don't hang up.

Instead, I hear myself explain in a half-whisper that I'm at work and can't talk, hoping the rows of pharmaceuticals and cough syrups muffle my voice.

"If you give me your name and number, I'll have someone call you at home tonight," says the woman on the other side.

And just like that, I find myself giving this stranger my name and phone number. What has gotten into me?

That night, my behavior surprises me even more. For some reason, I go home after work instead of stop at the bar like every other night. Just like the woman on the phone had promised, my home phone rang.

"My name is Dan," a kind voice explains. "And if you have a problem with alcohol, I want you to know, you are not alone."

From here, Dan begins to share his own story with alcohol. How it had both run him and ruined his life for years, how he had felt powerless to stop it. I'm completely mesmerized. This total stranger is telling me the intimate details of his addiction to alcohol. But his story is my story. How can this be true? Until now, I'd been certain I was the only one who had suffered this way.

Dan asks me to stay sober for 24 hours. I don't know if I can. Generally, it takes all the strength I can muster to claw my way through the work day without alcohol, let alone pills. I hadn't passed 24 whole hours without alcohol or drugs in four years. But in this moment, listening to Dan, after crying out for God's help and receiving Fred's candid reflection that morning, I know with all my heart that I really want to try. Dan tells me he'll meet me the next evening in the parking lot at a group meeting where I'll meet other people like him, people who understand my struggle. People who had gotten help.

At the end of that call, I feel myself surrounded by a pocket of goodness. I'd never spoken to anyone about the intimate details of my problems with alcohol before now. In fact, I hadn't even admitted them to myself. Hearing Dan talk does something to me. For the next 24 hours, I don't drink or drug. Only one day before, I couldn't have even imagined doing this. But now I feel myself held by something I cannot name, something that cushions me from the familiar craving and pain.

The next night I meet Dan in the parking lot of the O'Fallon Trailer Group because I'm terrified to walk into the meeting alone. I find a seat as close to the door as was available in case I want to leave.

I find myself in a room full of people who are all telling my story, just as Dan had the night before on the phone. For the first time, I hear people talking about the same confusion, hurt, shame, and self-hatred that had dogged me for so many years. Hearing other people give those feelings a name starts doing something to me. All these years, I believed myself insane. But other people, sane-looking people from every kind of background, age, ethnicity, class, or economic strata, are talking about the same experience.

As I listen and feel every nerve in my body awaken to the possibility of a solution, I hear that I'll need to admit to myself that I'm an alcoholic and that my life has become unmanageable. As I hear these words, I flash on the wild, unmanageable nature of my life, and yet am still in doubt that alcoholism is the cause of my craziness.

But I gained a measure of hope at the meeting that I never dreamed possible. Hope that I can recover, hope that I'm not crazy, hope that life really *would* get better from that day forward.

That night, I meet a woman named Mary. She takes me home and lets me talk. For hours, I talk. I vomit up my story, the pain I've never shared with anyone. No matter what I say, Mary listens. Finally, I've found a space to express myself.

I'm 25 years old and it's June in sweltering southern Illinois. After the first 24 hours pass, I realize I'll have to work hard at not drinking. At least I hope I can. But I also realize that I want sobriety more than I've ever wanted anything in my life. So many other people I'd just met are doing it. For the first time since I was 12 years old, I experience a sense of true belonging.

The next weeks are excruciating. My coworkers find me curled up in the back of the pharmacy... raw nerves, constipated, shaking, and aching. My body is screaming and fighting with itself as all parts of me are trying to find their way back to their healthy function.

I hadn't picked up a drink after that first meeting in June, but I understand so little about addiction that I don't even realize until a few months later that sobriety encompasses not just alcohol but also any kind of drugs. And I don't only want sobriety, I want all of the insanity to end. I finally find the courage to let go of anything and everything in order to find my way to full sanity.

So on August 11, 1979, I truly become clean and sober.

I learn as I'm sitting in meetings that admitting that I'm an alcoholic and that my life has become unmanageable would be a process that wouldn't take place overnight; rather over days, months, and years as the brain fog clears and I work a program of recovery.

In time, 30 hours of full sobriety becomes 30 days, then 60, then 90. Milestones like these don't just glide past me. Each one I celebrate, like reaching another peak in an arduous, uphill climb. They matter more to me than the G.E.D. I'd earned, more than my job or my little apartment. They mean I might not be crazy after all. That life might turn out to be worth living.

Lesson & Blessing

#7

Spotting Miracles

People in recovery usually introduce themselves with, "Hello, my name is _____, and I'm an alcoholic/drug addict/etc." When we say this, we're not claiming that we'll be prisoners forever of the full force of addiction. But we also don't fool ourselves into thinking that our addiction to the substance will ever be completely eliminated. As we explored in *Lesson & Blessing #6*, once the pathways in the brain are formed, they always have a tripwire. To deny this is not just naive, it's asking for trouble.

To get beyond addiction to drugs and alcohol, I had to hit bottom, and it's amazing to me that my bottom wasn't the worst thing that had ever happened to me. Instead, it was the extent of the shame I felt when someone I admired so much called me out regarding my drinking behavior. That last night I drank, Fred said I was a drunk and needed help. Because of my admiration for him, his raw words to me took me to my knees.

More than once, I've looked for a logical explanation for how I found myself on the phone with a woman from an answering service for Alcoholics Anonymous, just hours after Fred had shared his disgust with my drinking. Before the woman at the other end of that line had spoken, I'd never heard of 12-step programs, not even once. Maybe I'd jumbled the numbers when I dialed ADCO. Or maybe I misread the phone book. After all, the two names were fairly close to one another in the yellow pages, alphabetically speaking. My eyes could have skipped down a few lines.

Looking back, however, I know that something bigger had a hand in what took place that day in the pharmacy. Something bigger had a hand in the sequence of events leading up to that moment. Considering what would come from my involvement with A.A. in the years ahead, I could even call this mis-dial not an accident, but a miracle. I now believe that something bigger than me had been answering my prayers all along, and at this point I began noticing small, unexplainable events. This surprising moment of divine intervention would prove to be the largest miracle in my life, setting in motion countless more miracles to come. Abstinence and recovery began to create new neural pathways in my brain, slowly making the addictive pathways obsolete, unless I were to use again.

Thus, discovering this world of people who were willing and ready to help me, not just once but every single day, was essential for recovery. The miracle these people offered would unfold quietly, the way a tree grows and spreads. Being in meetings helped me finally figure out what I really thought and felt, simply because the people there gave me permission to talk long enough to learn how to hear my own mind and heart. The tears I'd bottled would spill, and keep on spilling, for longer than I even knew could be possible. For years, I would cry at every single meeting I attended, at a time when I attended a meeting every single day. But that didn't matter to the people in meetings. They let me be wrecked and heartbroken. They let me be ecstatic and elated. Whatever I brought, they said yes. I learned in time that I didn't need alcohol to manage my feelings, thanks to the space of that generous, open, yes.

Beyond the permission to explore my inner landscape, I'd also discovered the miracle of other people who had actually accomplished this thing that seemed so impossible—the thing they called recovery. I met people with stories even more grizzly than my own who had logged decades of sobriety. And this miracle, the hard-won miracle of their perseverance, gave a boost to my own.

Still, these miracles baffled me. Getting clean was

tough enough, but *staying* clean, though—damn, this took everything I had, and some things I didn't. No wonder I tried everything else first. Could I ever achieve this huge feat that others had? Especially in those early days, I swung back and forth between the poles of hope and despair like a circus performer on a trapeze.

So the most important miracles happened behind my eyes. These were miracles of mindset, an instant when my perspective would shift. In a meeting, someone might say something that would cascade through me—aha!—helping me understand something I'd been feeling for years but couldn't articulate. In a moment like this, I saw my life, and my past, differently.

I liken this to climbing a mountain. As I ascended, I continued to see more and more of what I'd left behind. The further I rose, the bigger my viewpoint became. Eventually, the small shifts, fruits of the effortful step-by-step-by-step of showing up differently in my life completely changed the landscape inside me. I began to rise out of the suffering I'd created.

The road ahead, the one that had appeared as magically as Dorothy's yellow bricks, wouldn't be easy on me. So many lessons awaited... little time bombs of struggle or pain. But these always popped open into the relief of more understanding or awareness. My life kept getting bigger, wider, and fuller, in proportion to the effort I invested in my transformation.

I call this the *Art of Recovery*, the unglamorous but highly rewarding reality of using the muscles of hope and faith to lean into, and live into, a miracle.

I can imagine you might be wondering how. I have learned that HOW stands for honesty, open-mindedness, and willingness. There is something greater than me that I claim is in all of us that supports the sincere cry of one's soul. Together, we'll discover that it's also in you.

Answered Prayer

*"There are more Tears shed over answered prayers
than unanswered prayers."*
~ Saint Teresa of Avila

At my very first meeting of my recovery program, I meet Marty Hubbard. I awkwardly shake his hand, and my vulnerable, shaky, terrified self can barely eke out a hello. I'm frozen and can barely speak to anyone, let alone this bigger-than-life human. A handful of practiced words thrown into the space between us—I can feel his warmth, his care I desperately want to trust and believe. I'm in awe that he would even stop and meet me... that he seems to not be judging me for crying through the entire meeting. Not in a million years can I imagine that this brief introduction will change my life.

At the end of the gathering, Marty approaches me with a big blue book against his chest. "This is the Big Book," he explains, "something like the 12-step scriptures, full of everything you need to begin recovery." Leaning toward me, Marty opens the book to its first blank page. Here, he points to a spot where he had scrawled out his and his wife's names and phone number in blocky letters.

"You call me or my wife if you ever need anything," he says. With that, we exchange a few more pleasantries, then he disappears once again into the blur of unknown faces.

That night, I sit in Mary's kitchen, spilling out my story. Marty goes on a shelf in the back of my mind.

Still, I don't forget what Marty said. I *do* need help, plenty of times in the weeks after that first meeting. The thought of his phone number, slanting upward in blue pen on its own page in my Big Book, comes to mind more than once as I struggle through the first months of recovery. I open the book to that page when I pick it up, looking at the number again before I begin reading from the text. I *want* to call Marty, like he'd suggested, yet I'm afraid. After so many years of going it alone and beating myself up, I still can't believe that anyone *really* wants to help me.

Not until one Sunday afternoon in late fall of my first year of recovery do I work up the nerve to call Marty. As always, Sundays make the loneliness of my life hurt the worst! That particular Sunday, it's bad enough for me to finally dial his number.

After a few rings, a woman answers. "Marty's not home right now," she explains when I ask for him. "But he should be here soon. He's told me all about you. Why don't you come on down?"

This is my first conversation with Dotty, Marty's wife. The idea of showing up at the home of a man I barely know when he won't even be there, makes me uncomfortable. But Dotty seems so kind.

Before I can think it through, I hear myself accepting her offer.

I arrive at their home not long after. Turns out, they live on the same side of the same street one mile west of my apartment in a two-story house with a big front porch and dormer window on top. For several years, I'd been passing their home without even realizing the miracle that lie inside.

Anxiously, I knock at the door. By now I've encountered Marty enough in meetings to know that I respect what he has to say, and I have an intuitive sense that I can trust him. But I have no idea what I'll find on the other side of that door.

"Come on in," Dotty greets me warmly.

Her friendly invitation seems genuine. But that door she stands behind looks more like a wall to me, a huge barrier I have to work up the courage to cross. I'm entering someone's home, and she's inviting me in with warmth and grace. There's no tumultuousness in the background, only the aroma of the next family meal filling the air. But

I don't yet trust it. Could I ever deserve to have something like this myself? Self-loathing and grief fight against my longing to step onto the ledge of her kindness.

Once inside, I'm in wonder of this homey, 1950's craftsman-style house—staircase to the right, foyer with a desk, light and airy kitchen, formal dining room that I later learn is full of family and friends more often than not.

Little do I know how many more afternoons—as well as mornings, evenings, weekends, and holidays—I'll spend like this one with Marty and Dotty. It takes time for me to trust that they can truly love me, not because of anything they do; but because of the suspicion I harbor that someday, once they know the real me, they'll change their minds and stop being so nice to me.

That day never comes. I find myself at Marty and Dotty's house more and more frequently over the following months, and I marvel at the love and acceptance they continue to lavish on me and all those they embrace. I begin coming to their house every day, and then twice a day—morning and evening. I share breakfast and dinner with Dotty, Marty, Grandma Danley (Dotty's mom), and Ellen and Charlie—two of their eight children who still live at home. From the beginning, this couple treats me like their long-lost daughter.

Leaving addiction behind means so much more than putting aside a bottle or a pill. By entering recovery, I learn or relearn nearly every part of my life. Even the simplest tasks—making decisions, shopping for groceries, fixing dinner, or even just dressing myself—these tasks I don't yet know how to do without alcohol and drugs.

This doesn't phase Marty and Dotty one bit. Dotty had entered a 12-step program for family and friends of those with alcohol or drug addiction about ten years before Marty had gotten sober. And both have been involved with the process of recovery—their own and that of the many people they support—long enough to understand how challenging it can be. On any given day, I might show up at breakfast in tears, only to come back for dinner beaming with a smile. When we talk, I describe the whole series of emotional ups and downs that has colored my day, which feels like being on a teeter-totter with someone twice my weight. But Marty and Dotty know that this kind of emotional turbulence comes with the territory. They listen patiently without trying to change me.

They also have a darn good time together. Humor takes center stage in how they relate to each other, even in small ways. Comic moments with them come often, moments like the afternoon when Marty comes home from work just as Dotty begins hanging a picture in their living room.

"Here, give me that," Marty says as he enters. After all, he's a handyman. He could take care of this.

"Okay," Dotty agrees. I'm sure Marty doesn't notice the sly smile on her face as she steps into the kitchen. *I* do, though. Secretly, she pulls me close, throwing her arm over my shoulder to turn us into a huddle. "Watch this," she whispers loudly, glancing over her shoulder toward the living room.

Just then, we hear a loud bang, followed swiftly by an even louder, "Ow!" Dotty and I snicker. So much for the man of the house saving the day.

I love the way Dotty handles it. In the end, she hangs the picture. But even though she had sensed it would turn out this way, she makes space for Marty to handle things the way he wants. She teases and plays with him instead of criticizing, and he responds in kind. Their lighthearted banter gives me a new version of marriage to consider, one entirely different from the contention-filled space between my own parents.

Because I'm in recovery, my family begins to settle down and they stop worrying about whether I'm dead or alive. My parents are divorced by now and I'm having a relationship with each of them on their own. My recovery program tells me it's my responsibility to begin healing the relationships with each of my parents and Ron, and I'm beginning to do that by learning from Dotty how to be a real daughter. I see my parents occasionally on weekends for brief hellos and call regularly to check in. I'm still harboring a lot of anger and resentment, and Marty and Dotty remind me that time heals.

Once I let myself lean into the caring I see between Marty and Dotty, I learn that I can count on them to help me find my way through my own problems. When I come through the door in tears, Dotty hands me a spoon, pointing to the pot I should stir, and continues chopping vegetables as I sob my way through the latest tragedy. "What are we going to do about it?" Dotty says to me as my story winds itself down. That "we" makes all the difference for me. "We" are in this together. "We" will figure it out. I'm not going it alone anymore.

More than once, I put that "we" to the test. One day just nine months after I get sober, I find myself walking with a friend through the streets of Belleville, Illinois, on one of those perfect afternoons—the temperature just right, tree branches swaying in a gentle breeze, and the whole world draped in golden, gauzy light. Giddy with the pleasure of both wandering aimlessly and doing it together, the two of us stumble upon a storefront display with a large, filigree photo in an ornate gold frame. The woman in the picture is proudly showing off her many tattoos.

Of course, neither of us had ever harbored any interest before that moment in getting a tattoo. It's 1980 and we live in conservative Illinois. Skin art is *not* in vogue. Bikers and sailors get tattoos, not young ladies.

I'm sure this explains why this storefront grabs us. The woman in the picture, unusually beautiful and oozing with confidence, looks down at us with a bravado and dare that we want to believe that we too, possess. Before long, we push through the glass door to find ourselves in an easy, fun conversation with the tattooed lady. She's even cooler in person than in the photo.

Before long, I'm gritting my teeth as the painted lady needles her colors onto my left breast.

It doesn't take long for me to regret my impulsive decision. In shock, I amble through the streets to my car. By the time I get to the Hubbard house, tears streak my face. More tears come as Dotty greets me.

"I got a tattoo!" I confess, the words bursting out of me like water breaking a dam.

"Are you okay?" Dotty wants to know. She seems less concerned about the tattoo than she is about me.

Had she heard me correctly? "Yes, I'm okay," I sob, still unable to put into words the tangled mix of emotions competing inside me. It had seemed so right to get the tattoo when I did it, so liberating. After all, why should I let all the stupid social rules dictate my behavior? But now, I'm beginning to understand these rules and in some cases even see their value for my life. Despite not being a user anymore, emotionally speaking, I still have one foot in each world. Maybe Dad had it right—*I don't have any goddamn brains.*

"You want to talk to Marty?" Dotty asks, aware of how much it soothes me to hear his advice. "He's not here, but let's call him together." The notion of embracing this next life challenge *together* brings an instant relaxation.

Before he'd gotten sober, Marty had lived through his own escapades. He relished retelling stories from that time, tales like the time he won a coffin in a card game. How he had showed up after-hours with the thing in tow, and Dotty didn't blink an eye. This was just how he rolled.

On the phone, Marty asks, "What's wrong, Little Bit?" He had christened me with this nickname early on and I loved it. At 5'1" and 95 pounds, I fit the bill. Marty understands that despite my chronological age, I feel like a little child still growing up on the inside.

Words splutter out of me: "I got a tattoo."

Calmly he asks, "Where?"

"On my left breast."

Without missing a beat, Marty says, "Well, it can't be too damned big," as he chuckles at himself out loud.

Even though their consistent acceptance comes so freely, I continue to struggle to count on this love from Marty and Dotty over the weeks and months ahead. Deep inside, I wonder if I can really afford to open my heart. Will I just get hurt all over again?

To truly understand this truth, I would need another 18 years of practice. But my journey to that place of freedom began as Marty and Dotty passed a hashbrown and cheese casserole across their dinner table to me.

Lesson & Blessing

#8

My Life Is an Answered Prayer

Luckily, though, I *did* open my heart—slowly at first, and more with time. Dotty and Marty taught me how to date, how to cook, and how to talk and think like a young woman with integrity. They showed me how to scale the rocky crags of my psyche without losing sight of mundane tasks. But one of the most important lessons they taught me was how to allow myself to be loved.

The blessing of their love would change me dramatically. For at least half of my life, I'd yearned for a family that reflected what I believed love could truly look like and a place I could truly belong. With them, I found both. Day by day, Marty and Dotty exemplified what love-in-action looked and felt like. My family had *told* me that they loved me, but I wasn't often *shown* what love was, so I couldn't feel it or develop it for myself. Witnessing their family's unconditional love for one another—and for me—gave me glimpses of what was possible until I got strong enough to begin developing love for myself.

In all my addictions, I'd been searching for the belonging that "family" represented to me in my mind. Not only the roles I saw portrayed on TV sitcoms or in the relationship between my mother and father, but what I longed for was an authentic relationship where I could experience what I'd seen modeled by Marty and Dotty. I'd been raised to become a wife and a mother and ached for the opportunity to both love and be loved. This desire for the family I never had as a kid wore a groove in my heart so deep that it became an unspoken prayer.

Even though they were devout Catholics, Marty and Dotty never shamed or blamed me for the choices I made, even the choices that were as the result of my cultural conditioning. Previous to meeting their version of God, I'd known only a punishing source. Being around them also taught me a different relationship to the religion and God I'd grown up with. It was becoming obvious to me that the miracles showing up in my life were proof of a higher power that had always been there for me.

My life with Marty and Dotty might not have fit the cultural idea of a family, but it was another answer to an unspoken prayer. It filled holes in the parenting from my own father and mother that I needed in order to grow up on the inside. For my development, I truly needed this kind of support. Since age 12, when I began drinking, I hadn't matured internally. My emotional growth had come to a halt when I became addicted to alcohol, a condition that's true for any form of mind-altering addiction. On the outside, I'd been going through the motions, doing my very best to imitate the way I thought the adults around me or the ones I saw on TV behaved; but on the inside, I saw life through the eyes of a terrified little girl.

Marty and Dotty's love for each other and for me gave me a family feeling of belonging and laid a foundation upon which I could rebuild my ideas of what family could be.

What a surprise to discover that the answer to my plea for a home and belonging had been waiting for me just one mile down my own street. I'd driven past Marty and Dotty's house as a matter of routine, long before we met. But until I reached a place of surrender to my addictions, they might as well have lived on the moon. In a way, they had. In the throes of addiction, The Land of Recovery lie far beyond my reach.

In time, I've come to see that my life is an answered prayer—and always was. In order to actually experience my life this way, however, I have to live from a mindset that intends to access the reality of this truth. I must practice hope, before faith, and that the pureness of a prayer is already available. Hope is what I gathered at my first meeting—that recovery is possible; then faith came as the result of using the tools and seeing the sustained changes in others and myself. Then I began keeping my eyes peeled for the miracles that are all around me. Within this awareness, as I hone my attention and look back through my life, I can see that even during my worst moments before and during my addictions, my prayers were being answered, unbeknown to me.

To this day, this knowing has become my own North Star. When I find myself with a prayer, a yearning, a desire, I remind myself: *My life is an answered prayer*. I repeat this to myself to dissolve the fears that rise up in me. I use it to let go of my preconceived ideas about what the answer to my prayer will look like.

We often try to figure out the answer to the prayer, but this is a little like connecting the dots in the picture books when we were kids. When we begin, we think we know what the picture is going to look like; but by the end, the wholeness of the image always comes together in (often) delightfully un-expected ways. Over time, we learn to trust the process.

When things get hard in the moment, I coach myself: *Take a breath. There's another miracle just around the corner.* Then I step back and watch for the answer that comes from people, places, and things that enlighten me to what else is present and possible... another dot in the larger picture. The answer comes. It always comes... in ways that strengthen my belief that I'm always guided and taken care of by unseen forces, my higher power.

So, I implore you to take steps that are perhaps the op-posite of what your habituated behavior would have you to do. Trust in the "usual unusual" process. We try to second-guess what's good for us or what's going to happen if we take a step that is out of the norm. Miracles come in quiet whis-pers and unusual opportunities. You can easily talk yourself out of trusting them because you *think* you know what's best for you. Your best thinking has gotten you only to where you are now, so you may need to live outside the box!

Your unanswered prayer is the quiet cry of your soul that actually knows what's best for you.

Awakening

*"You learn who you are by unlearning
who they taught you to be."*
~ Nikki Rowe

"Casablanca." This old movie belongs to my father's generation. But a stylish hair salon bearing the same name had cropped up in the area where I live, and it fits me perfectly. Its owner, my friend Getta, oozes style and sex appeal (Mick Jagger had wanted to date her!), and she had infused the salon with them. A black-and-white color scheme plays against vintage details, an echo of the old romance movie that had inspired the theme. Lazy ceiling fans give the place a breezy feel. At the door, a friendly receptionist offers coffee, tea, or water with the air of a dignified concierge. Touches like these make it unique for a salon in the late-70's. An appointment at Casablanca feels like a getaway to me.

Only a month into my own process of recovery (even before I had been to Marty and Dotty's house), I walked into Casablanca for an appointment for a haircut. Since high school, when my mom's friend had badly burned my hair with a home perm, I'd become very particular about who could even touch my head. Luckily, I'd scheduled with Getta. I trust her with my hair completely—no small matter for me.

But when I arrive for my appointment with her, I find out that Getta has gone home sick for the day. The receptionist wants to know, am I willing to let her newest husband, whom I'd never met, cut my hair instead?

I barely agree to this arrangement. I must be under some sort of spell, the same one that had prompted me to accidentally contact a 12-step program instead of ADCO only a handful of weeks before.

Almost the moment I sit down in his chair, my hair stylist's husband, Dennis, begins telling me about Eckankar, a body of spiritual teachings built on the notion that the soul is eternal and exists because God loves it. According to Eckankar, we're all taking a journey of Self- and God-realization, which we can accelerate through conscious contact with Spirit. By exploring the spiritual world through soul travel, dreams, and other techniques, we can have spiritual experiences and a closer relationship with God.

Flash.

Light bursts through the darkness of my world like a camera's bulb flooding a dusky landscape. As Dennis tells me of Eckankar, I catch a series of breathtaking glimpses of a vast landscape beyond the borders of Catholicism and the staunch German values of my community.

Who knew that all my life, this is what I'd really been yearning for: a chance to investigate new ideas, explore curiosities, learn and question about the God that I would come to know.

Perhaps I'd always known about it, from a place in me without any words. Everything about what Dennis is sharing sounds right to me, like remembering.

I want more.

I go home and fervently begin studying Eckankar. I live in the conservative Midwest of the late 1970's, and Dennis is the first person I know who's studying anything remotely like Eckankar. So I keep my interest under wraps. But this doesn't stop me from sneaking away to St. Louis at least once a month, sometimes more often, to join an Eckankar study group that meets regularly.

With Dennis as my mentor, I begin a five-plus-year study of Eckankar. This study ushers me into a new way of understanding the world and my place in it, one that would guide me for the rest of my life. Something exists beyond me, something they call "consciousness." I learn that life holds more, so much more than what I can see with my eyes alone. I'm introduced to karma, spiritual freedom, and how to "become a co-worker with God."

Shortly after I first meet Dennis, I pull out of the parking lot after a recovery meeting where I hear once again that it's necessary for me to believe that a power greater than me will return me to sanity, and to turn my will over to said being. The only way I find the strength to take these second and third steps is alone inside my Firestone red Chevy Camaro screaming at the top of my lungs: *I don't know who you are! I don't know where you are, but I'm ready to believe!* I suddenly realize that perhaps this higher power, this *Presence*, had already been known to me.

As the teachings of Eckankar and my burgeoning relationship with a non-Catholic power greater than me seep into my soul, I now begin to realize that my body needs support. Cute and petite, I get plenty of attention from men, as well as approval—or jealousy—from women. But so many years of alcohol and drugs have taken their toll. No matter what anyone comments about my appearance, I suspect my body's insides have not fared the storms of addiction well.

Along with this, I now find myself with a lot of free time on my hands. Since age 12, drugs and alcohol had taken up most of my extra time. What can I do with myself now that won't send me right back to bottles, pills, and needles?

An old boyfriend of mine is working as a furniture mover. One day, he shows me the body mechanics of how to properly lift heavy objects. With this simple act, another light bulb comes on. I realize that when I lift something this way, a feeling comes over me, a sense of my own strength and empowerment.

I take this simple recognition as a clue and start lifting weights.

Exercise is now just coming in vogue. Women in thong leotards line up daily along neat rows of fake stairs for step aerobics at the Vic Tanny gym I joined. But instead of skin-tight Lycra in pink and baby blue, I suit up in baggy t-shirts and slouching gym shorts. I walk past the Jazzercise classes, down the hall, and into a large, airless room lined with racks of barbells, free weights, and slanting vinyl benches. Here, grunting—not dancing—fills the room.

I don't need very long to discover that Tom Stock, a USA heavyweight lifting champion, is working out regularly in this little room. What he lacks in traditional good looks, this strapping Midwestern type makes up for in brute strength. Because he takes the sport seriously, he often coaches and trains admirers who apply themselves with the same gusto. More than my own looks, I think my commitment and follow-through with training get his attention. He agrees to coach me.

Of course, I'm not entering weightlifting with any ambition to compete. I'm looking for a way to keep myself from drinking or drugging. But Tom pushes and supports me in his typical 80's-guy, not-touchy-feely way. And I find myself fascinated with the way the body works and with finding out how to get it to do something that seems impossible. I measure just 5'1" and now weigh 110 pounds, so Tom calls me *Little Linda*. Yet he never sees my size as a handicap. At his urging, I soon find myself lifting weights competitively.

Three or four times a week, I carefully load weight racks for the routine Tom sets for me. The long bar I use for free-weight lifting weighs 35 pounds before I even add any plates to it. With a new routine, I start adding light weights to the bar and work up. After more practice, I sometimes attempt so much weight in one lift that I need one of the men to spot me in case I can't keep it up. When someone in our room lifts this way, no one speaks. No one wants to distract a fellow lifter from the intense level of focus a moment like this requires.

I feel the potent mix of endorphin euphoria and muscle exhaustion that runs through my body at the end of a hard session. Rivulets of sweat stream down my back, my arms, and my neck as I slowly drag the plates, one by one, back to their storage areas.

No other women in the gym are powerlifting. Until now, I'd obediently stuck to my role as a prissy Catholic girl, staying within the gender-prescribed lanes of that culture. Without meaning to, though, I'd joined an all-boys club, one without a single other female member. Luckily, this rough-and-tumble crowd, if gruff at times, focuses on lifting, not flirting. They treat me like a fellow athlete, not a potential date.

Competitive powerlifting provides me more benefits than I could have ever imagined. For one thing, its demands on my schedule tremendously support my recovery from addiction. In my 12-step community, I'm one of the youngest people getting sober. I have few people my age to hang out with who understand my life. But the rigorous, regular practice that my world-class coach insists on gives me a positive alternative to rejoining the drinking and drugging crowd I know so well.

As I become more invested in my training regimen, I also give up smoking and begin running 10k races. In weightlifting, I gradually reclaim my physical health from the effects of addiction.

Weightlifting is giving me more than just a toned physique. As I train, I learn to compete against myself, challenging my body to go further, push harder, than ever before. I begin to understand a power inside me that has nothing to do with muscles or good looks. Lifting weights puts me in a zone, a mental state where I draw strength from somewhere deep within myself. Without meaning to, I've found another meditation practice.

I become mesmerized by the power of concentration. To harness this power, I develop discipline—a quality I'd never cared about until now. The sport is teaching me that success begins in the mind, not the physical world of things.

One weekend, my weightlifting buddies invited me to join them at the Creve Coeur Lake boating races. I hadn't spent much time with them outside of the gym and don't really know what to expect. But I'm thrilled at the prospect of a social outing! Even though I still have no idea how to navigate my life without alcohol, I ache for a chance to spend time with folks my own age outside of a 12-step meeting.

I soon discover, however, that my new friends don't share my own aspirations to sobriety. As I step into their van, the aroma of booze slaps me awake. For the first time since I'd gotten clean, I'm in a social setting saturated with alcohol. Even though none of my fellow passengers are drunk yet, everyone is drinking, including the driver.

Why hadn't I seen this coming? Of course everyone's drinking. How else do macho weightlifters blow off steam if not with a round of beers? Still, even if I'd anticipated some drinking, which I somehow hadn't, I didn't expect them to be drinking so heavily long before the event has even begun.

I find myself clutching the seat in front of me all the way to the lake, terrified we'll all die in an accident. Even worse, the people who will later find me dead will think *I* had been drunk. Watching them kick back beers while we're at the lake, I shudder to consider the ride back home.

On our journey home, we gained another passenger, Jeff, a handsome guy about my age, mid-20's. He reminds me of... someone, a movie star, though I can't put my finger on whom at first. Eventually it hits me, though. He looks just like Gonzo, the sexy, young medical assistant played by Gregory Neale Harrison in the popular TV series, "Trapper John, M.D."

Besides his good looks, I immediately notice he isn't drinking as much as the other guys. I quietly confess my fear to him: that this ride could be our last. Since he'll be getting out of the van sooner than the others on the way home, he suggests I get off with him.

One year later (just shy of my second recovery anniversary), I find myself standing on ten heavily wooded acres outside of St. Louis: Jeff's land. By then, we'd moved in together. Now Jeff is explaining his vision for the home he'd build here. A road over there, a barn right here, a house bermed into the side of the hill just down there. He plans to build it himself.

I'm in awe. Jeff loves photography, nature, and skiing. Heck, he loves life, and he has so many interests. And this good-looking gentleman loves *me*.

Of course, I find this hard to believe. On the outside, my life has changed significantly, and continues to change more and more every day. On the inside, though, I still feel the wounding of my past and am experiencing its continued effects on my body, emotions, and mind. I had shot dope, pilfered drugs from a pharmacy, stolen money from my own family. I'd lied and cheated and used people. Though all of this had happened in the past, my shame about it feels as vivid as if I'd just come down off a high. I feel terrified I will mess up again, so I berate myself for every little mistake.

In sharp contrast, Jeff treats me with affection and respect. *Do I really deserve this?*

If my time with the Eckankar community was giving me a new *understanding* of the world, my experiences with Jeff taught me how to *see* the world differently. As we walk the land together, I get to learn the types of trees, slowing down enough to watch the deer and squirrels in their dance. This man carries inside himself a clear vision of his future. This feels like the beginning of a life with new possibilities and promise.

I realize that turning this newfound possibility into something tangible will require lots of hard work. My childhood of concrete and barbed wire, with one military base following the next, had done nothing to prepare me for a project like Jeff's. Build a passive solar house in the middle of the wilderness? Shoot, I'd never even so much as picked up a hammer. Secretly, being in nature this much makes me nervous, too. I feel a little bit like I'd just found myself plunked down in Moscow without speaking Russian. Sink or swim, I'm going to have to catch up as fast as I can.

But Jeff's passion inspires me to go beyond my fears. For the first time in my life, I buy a warm coat and flannel shirts, the sleeves of which I promptly roll up, and set to work.

To start, we rented a bulldozer and cleared the road leading into our property. This first day, I find myself pulling out heavy trees by hand. I tease Jeff that he had only fallen in love with me because I lift weights, so I can now lift trees.

Gusts of cool wind swirl leaves around our feet as we finish a full day of hard work one autumn afternoon. Jeff and I wrap up the day as we usually do, by walking the land together. I'd come to relish these walks with Jeff. Instead of fearing nature, I'd come to love being out in the forest. Even more, I love hearing Jeff talk about what he sees next for this place.

Today, Jeff tells me he has a surprise for me. As we walk, he begins asking pointed questions: *Where do I see myself in the years ahead? What do I want from my life?*

Sitting down on a log to rest, we continue the conversation. As I ponder these questions, I feel both the tension and delight at the thought of having a chance at a normal life with such a caring man.

I must have given him the right answers. Pulling a ring from his blue jean pocket, he asks, "Will you spend the rest of your life with me?" In my work boots and jeans, I happily accept his proposal of marriage.

I'd been raised to one day get married. I'd even dreamed of it. But never had I summoned the courage to imagine myself marrying a man like Jeff. Often quiet and serious, he also has a sarcastic side that surfaces unexpectedly and makes me laugh. He embodies stability and reliability, both emotionally and financially, and he doesn't have an alcohol or drug addiction. Also high on my list, he was, what we referred to in the 80's as "a hunk." On top of all that, my parents love him. I can hardly believe my luck.

On a perfect spring day—March 13, 1982—with me just two and a half years sober, Jeff and I marry. To please our parents, we hold a modest Catholic wedding, including a round of confessions that Jeff's mother had slyly wiggled us into at the last minute. But I don't mind. I'm marrying the man of my dreams. All the rest are mere details.

Now I can really see a new future for myself, one so different from the history that I'd been delivered from. But on a practical level, our life doesn't change much. We continue building the house, using only cash to pay for the project, which we work on during evenings and weekends while maintaining full-time jobs. Once we complete the shell of the home to keep out the elements, we move in and keep on working.

On an internal level, too, I'm building, growing, changing. I continue going to both 12-step and Eckankar groups, and at home I read Jeff's copies of Mother Earth News from cover to cover. My relationship with Jeff is stabilizing me, giving me a glimpse of what a "normal" life looks like. Just as I'm learning how to use a hammer, a chainsaw, and a drill, I also learn how to use mental tools to reshape my thinking. From the raw material of new ideas, I begin framing an internal structure for a life that has a foundation of substance.

And building the house only deepens the lessons in focus and determination that weightlifting had begun. One afternoon, Jeff and I plan to use our 240 International tractor with a front loader to rake gravel over the plumbing we had laid over the house's 60- by 30-foot footprint. Unfortunately, it had been raining for a week—no chance of using the tractor in weather like this. Instead, we drag gravel, one scuffed-up wheelbarrow at a time, over to the site, painstakingly covering the area by hand.

Sweat drips down my face as mosquitoes buzz around my entire body. They must know that my hands are too tied up to swat them away and they make a meal of any exposed skin. Over and over, I find myself chanting the serenity prayer, pulling up strength from somewhere deep within myself to complete this task.

Slowly but consistently, we fill in the rough sketch of Jeff's vision like hikers on a steep trail, one step following the next. If we can't see the end of the project just yet, at least we know we'll get there eventually. Until then, we enjoy the scenery.

As the house begins to take shape, we discover that other people have bought land in this area with the same idea as Jeff's. We make connections with fellow readers of Mother Earth News who are also spending their free time building houses, just like us. Along with our shared interests, we all live far enough from town and its conveniences that we begin to genuinely need each other. In time, we support each other's visions and show up for one another's barn raisings. They become more than just neighbors; they are people I count on, and they count on me. I'm learning how to be a reliable friend. Another sense of belonging has somehow fallen at my feet.

Eight years of hard labor later, Jeff and I are beginning to put the finishing touches on the house. At one entrance, stained glass windows that Jeff and I had designed together cast colorful patterns over us as we enter. Once inside, vaulted ceilings and big picture windows create a sense of spaciousness and opening to a gorgeous view of the surrounding woods. The kitchen features cabinets of cherry that Jeff had made himself, and the master bathroom boasts handmade walnut cabinets and a sunken jacuzzi tub. We even put in a one-acre lake next to the house, which stands bermed into a hillside as though it had not been built, but rather, had sprouted from the land like one of the forest's trees. In the area, there is no house like it.

When I show others our place, people marvel over what Jeff and I have created together. They see the beauty of the place, its unique charm and value. But I see something different. For me, this house— or home—holds memories. It is a record of my life with Jeff, our lessons together, and what it's taken for us to make his dream a reality. For me, it serves not so much as a showpiece, but as a symbol... a representation of how far I've come, the life I've rebuilt.

Lesson & Blessing

#9

Have Faith in the Process

With the realization about how to properly lift heavy objects, I'd stumbled upon another key ingredient in getting free from alcohol and drugs. Addiction had happened in my body, not just my mind, and it needed to be healed there, too. As I've shared in previous chapters, addiction gets wired powerfully into the body's physiology. Like a tornado or a hurricane, it can also ravage bodily systems in a way that requires careful, ongoing repair.

In time, I would carry the focus and determination I gained from weightlifting into every part of my life. I not only began to heal my body, I began to discover my essence.

The first day of recovery, just one day without alcohol or drugs, had been a major accomplishment for me. When that turned into another day, and then another, I began to hope that my life could be different. Inside, I had decided: whatever pain it cost to get sober had to be less than the pain of my life so far. No matter what, I wouldn't turn back.

With this commitment, my life became an entirely new

experience. When I first stopped drinking and drugging, I had considered sobriety my endgame. Addiction had made me so myopic that I could see only through the lens of the substances I knew so well, even when working to get free from them.

But the longer I stayed clean, the more I discovered how much life had to offer. Books, conversations, ideas to consider, adventures to be had. Like veils over my eyes, drugs and alcohol had clouded my vision. Now those veils had fallen away.

Still, I'd spent so many years blind. Seeing this new world around me didn't bring only joy. Without drugs, I had no way to numb my sorrows. Now, instead of pushing them away, I had to move toward them. I was learning to embrace all facets of my experience—a worthy task, though hardly an easy one.

Awakening came in bursts, small at first, like a flash bulb flaring in a dark room. Click—I see! Then dark again. But the moments of understanding grew as I did. Without realizing it, I was teaching myself how to come out of the shadowy world I'd always known and live in one with colors, textures, and beauty.

As I think of this time in my life, I often remember the lessons I received from building the house. During one phase of construction, Jeff and I would drive our truck over bumpy dirt roads to an old coal strip mine. Here, we filled the truck bed with large, heavy stones meant for a retaining wall that would flank either side of the house, holding back the berm behind it.

I loved watching Jeff work on this. Piece by piece, he would fit the stones into place, trying one, then another. I watched him with fascination, but try as I might, I couldn't yet grasp his larger vision. Not until he had finished these walls would I understand where he had been going with his creation all along.

This illustrates perfectly the first ten years of my recovery, which included my marriage to Jeff. During that time, I was collecting experiences—large and small—trying each one out, experimenting with where to put them. I knew I was puzzling through something important. But I didn't know exactly what, not yet.

All these years later, however, I can see the bigger picture. The weightlifting, my exploration of spirituality, being married, and building a house—all of it added up to something more than the sum of its parts. As the building of my life took place alongside the building of our house, small flash points of awakening gradually came together in a larger vision, one that would eventually reshape my whole life in the years to come.

My cultural upbringing, societal messages, and early childhood experiences had me believe that success was about the number of years married to one person or holding down one job for my entire life. I'd lived for so long with an idea of the way life was *supposed* to look, instead of living one day at a time, one moment at a time. I learned this in recovery.

In life, we can't know how each experience will unfold our lives for the next, and the next. Because we often don't have faith in the process, we get overly focused on ourselves, wondering: *Am I doing it right?* Right now, whether you've ever been in recovery or not, you're probably judging something about your past based on the knowledge you have today. *If only I knew then what I know now!* We often think we should have done it differently, not realizing that exactly how we did it is the reason we have become the people we are today.

I've now learned that it's about the journey, not the arrival, and I invite you to this radical and extraordinary journey of living for each moment.

Making Amends

"Forgiveness is not an emotion.
It is a decision made by your whole self
after your true emotional work has been done."
~Karla McLaren

"If this is what sobriety has to offer, you can stick it up your ass," I say when called on by a chairperson at a meeting, my feet up on the table and my back to the front of the room. I'm such a mix of emotions—doubt, fear, anger, distrust—that this anger has become a control mechanism, and my terror of ever drinking and drugging again has me respond defensively.

When I'd first gotten sober, I listened to what other people said in meetings about life getting better all the time, and I would think, "Oh god, I hope that's true!" It's also what the *Presence* had said that day on the operating table, and I wanted to believe that a life beyond the hell I'd known could happen for me someday.

But it's now 1984, and I find myself still holding onto the guarantee that life will keep getting better if I would take the suggestions that were offered to me in the meetings. I'm 5 years sober and despite having met and married Jeff, I still have little direct experience with a sustained sense of inner peace and serenity. Others' stories mostly guide me forward. Can I actually experience a complete turnaround? Or will the demons of my past catch up with me, dragging me back into the inferno I'd escaped? I still carry too much grief, sadness, and confusion to feel goodness in myself for more than the flashes. Even while I hope for this sustained change, I continue to doubt I can actually achieve one. After all, I've only explored these new ways of being for a handful of years, which doesn't yet balance out the 15 I had as an addict.

To handle my fears, I get perfect. I attend at least one meeting every day, and I read my Big Book just as often. If my sponsor tells me to do something, I do even more than what she asks. I dive full force into the world of recovery, taking a job with a film production company that focuses exclusively on making movies to support recovery from alcoholism and drug addiction. I support a group of my various recovery connections to create a club in the building just next door to my work. Thanks to the close proximity, I can now attend as many as three meetings a day—and I often do.

Living this way starts to work wonders for me. After my extreme experience with alcohol and drugs, I need an extreme remedy. By saturating myself in this world, full of people who understand my past and can help me navigate my future, I begin to form a new way of seeing myself.

However, there's another underlying motivator for my perfectionism: the terror of relapse. My life on alcohol and drugs had been so awful that I never wanted to find myself back there again. I will do anything to keep from re-entering that vicious loop.

And in part, I'm aiming for perfection because I simply don't yet know how to live my life authentically. In childhood, I'd trained myself to mimic the people around me since my own honest expressions had never received much welcome. As an addict, I'd mimicked other addicts. Now, I mimic the people I meet at meetings, weaving their lingo into my own as I take my turn to share.

Fortunately, my recovery program begins to counterbalance the pattern of faking my way through life that I had developed to survive my childhood. "Bring the body," the old timers say to me, "and the mind will follow." I follow this advice on faith. But by bringing myself regularly to meetings, I learn the principles of recovery not as dogmas I'm to follow to gain the favor of God, but as life lessons. I listen to so many stories, many from people who have logged 20, 30, 40 years of sobriety. Through them, I experience vicariously the way the tenets of my program can change a person's life. My blind faith in the 12 steps begins to have some solid, proven truth for me.

The fourth step of recovery, which we read aloud at every

meeting, instructs me to make a fearless moral inventory of myself. How had I behaved? How has my behavior impacted other people? These questions, only I can answer.

The program goes one step further. I can't simply admit them to myself, I also need to have a witness and make a commitment to change my behavior in the future. Next come the sixth and seventh steps which have me own up to my character defects and shortcomings, and once again surrender to a higher power and ask to have them removed.

Then, I need to make amends.

I start this process first in meetings. Here, I find a safe audience. Many others speak about the past, including the pain they feel over the mistakes they had made under the influence of alcohol and drug addiction. A queasy feeling comes over me every time I speak about my own past. But even if I don't yet know the word for this emotion of shame, at least I know that I'm not the only person who experiences it.

Still, I begin to realize that confessing my mistakes to people who have been untouched by my actions will never close the door on my past. To truly recover, not just from using, but from the behavior patterns that had inspired me to use, I'm going to have to make a list of all the people I had harmed. Then, one by one, I'll need to make amends to all of them. And I know I have to choose carefully how, when, and if to make amends in order to do no additional harm.

Making amends has no script. True, I know I can practice what I need to say with another person... I can get suggestions and ideas from people who have gone down this road ahead of me. But facing someone I had harmed and admitting it, *that* I cannot fake. In these moments, I have to be the raw, imperfect version of myself.

This is when recovery gets real for me. I become real.

Taking responsibility for myself in this way, face-to-face with someone I've hurt, means I have skin in this game. I'm no longer simply watching from the bleachers of life. I begin getting scuffed up, failing, falling, and getting back up again.

This process forces me to look at my past from the perspective of the other people in it. I've now gone from chasing the next high, a state of mind in which nobody but me and my dope mattered, to actively thinking about other people. Caring about them. I've now entered another universe.

The list of people I've harmed seems endless. I sit in countless meetings and hear someone tell a story that sparks a memory of my own. Not *only* a memory, though. Another name—or two or three— that belongs on my list. I'm constantly stumbling over these land-mines of my past. Around every corner, it seems, one more person crouches, waiting to explode into my memory.

Luckily, my program teaches me how to engage this process gradually. First of all, I learned not to say, "I'm sorry," since I had said that so many times when I was using. My "sorry" had come to mean nothing. Instead, my first amends, the ones that I can handle, come in the form of living amends. Living amends arise from the way I change my actions. Without any words, my new life begins to speak to the responsibility I've taken for my past actions, as well as my commitment to show up differently in the present.

My own living amends begin surfacing naturally, in many ways that only the people closest to me can recognize. At the most basic level, I begin paying my bills on time. I show up for work on time every day. When I speak with my parents, I no longer cuss them out. I stop asking them for money and begin calling simply to ask how they're doing. Every time I spoke with Mom until this point, she would plead with me not to drink or drugs. For the first time, they no longer worry that my addiction will shake up their lives.

This change in me affects the whole dynamic of our family system. For most of my life, my brother had played the family hero. I, on the other hand, had served as the scapegoat. But I no longer fit that role. Because of my living amends, they can no longer point to someone—me—as the root of their personal or family problems. The space in our family that all my wild behavior had once occupied had ceased, and it's now left a blank spot.

To fill the blank spot, I don't say too much when offering my family living amends. To speak amends directly to them—the people I had hurt the most—is going to require a whole different level of strength and courage. I'm just not ready.

So I start making verbal amends by reconnecting with the people who had made a positive difference in my life. I go to Mrs. Bosworth, my high school psychology teacher. This woman had told me I was a good person, and I'd never forgotten her words. In fact, the memory had popped into my mind at my very worst moments and given me the courage to continue my recovery. So I make the trip back to her classroom to tell her how much this means to me.

Next, I find the phone number for Dr. William Smith and give him a call. To get me off the streets, this Emergency Room doctor would check me into the hospital and pump my body full of glucose to get my levels back up. The way he had cared for me, without judging me as an addict, instead seeing me as a real human being who needed his help—this had meant more to me than words could express. When I was still using, his face would pop into my mind. *If this doctor thinks I'm worth saving,* I would think, *then maybe I am.* When I call him, I thank him for saving my life. Without his help, I'm certain I would have left the Earth long before I even had a chance at recovery.

I also finally reach out to the psychiatrist who had first told me I was an alcoholic when I was 21—Dr. Robert Anderson. I had waited five years into my recovery to make this visit, not because I was too afraid to speak with him, but I had feared relapse and hadn't wanted to go until I was *truly* clean and sober. After five years, I finally trust that I've stably turned things around in my life. What a relief I feel to thank him for having told me the truth all those years ago. I share openly that I've finally begun to find my way forward, and I hope that my experience will help him in working with other patients like me.

I then work up the courage to actually make heart amends with people from my past I had wronged. In one form or another, I say to each of them, "These are the things I did, and I was wrong. I take responsibility for my past. Is there anything you need to say to me, or need from me?" Most say they simply need me to stay the course.

Sometimes I can't make amends directly with someone, either because I can't find the person, or because he or she has died. In these cases, I hold the intention that my new way of living, focused on integrity and helping others, serves as my best amends.

As I reach out to people, something surprising begins to happen. Nearly everyone I contact is genuinely happy to forgive and release me from past mistakes. Their forgiveness gives me permission to forgive myself. With each encounter, my own self-judgment gets lighter. And the more I release myself from mistakes, the more I begin to see *myself* in a different light. Perhaps I actually *can* become more than just an addict. Each act of making heart amends leaves me with a growing resolve to continue the change in my behavior that recovery had sparked.

Still, not every confrontation comes easily. Just as I had waited five years to talk to my former psychiatrist, I spent even longer agonizing over the reconciliation I needed to make with the owner of the pharmacy in Edgemont where I had daily stolen meds to support my habit. I had worked for Frank for five years total, two of those years as an addict, and three of them clean and sober, and I both like and respect him. I hate the idea of admitting to him that I had taken advantage of his good nature.

Even more compelling, though, is the terror that I'll end up in prison once I tell him exactly how I had behaved. The fear of incarceration for the various crimes I had committed while addicted runs constantly in the back of my mind.

I let seven years pass in recovery before I set up a meeting with Frank to make amends. Knowledge of what I had done at the pharmacy weighs so heavily on my soul, to the point that I've become willing to do whatever it takes to make amends. I have to free myself from the guilt I feel. Also, somewhere inside I realize I'm waiting until the statute of limitations has passed on my crime of stealing drugs before I take action.

Once I make the appointment to meet him at Fischer's Restaurant for lunch, I become a bundle of nerves. How will he respond? I had taken so many narcotics in my time there that I shudder to consider how long it will take to repay him. And he would be well within his legal rights to report me to the authorities. Maybe he would even see it as his responsibility to do so, considering I could be a danger to others.

At Fischer's, we find ourselves in a spacious dining room with a large fireplace at one end. A hostess seats us at one of many tables covered in white tablecloths, more than half of the tables full of customers, and we choose from a list of comfort foods that had made the place an area favorite: fried chicken, Reuben sandwiches, crispy-smooth French fries. I'd been coming here since high school, and the familiar, cozy atmosphere usually puts me a little at ease. But at this moment, I can't care less about food.

After I order something I know I probably won't be able to eat,

I make chit-chat with Frank about the weather, about what's happening in his life now. I'm stalling. When I had asked him to meet me for lunch, I hadn't confessed why I wanted to see him. Now I have to take the leap.

"Frank," I begin, gathering my strength, "I asked you to lunch because I owe you amends for my behavior during the first two years of working in your pharmacy. I need to share how that behavior affected our relationship and your trust in me."

Phew. I had started. But I still have plenty more to say, none of it easy.

In a shaky voice, I explain how I had stolen both drugs and money from the pharmacy, how I had used Valium® or Percocet® to get my nerves under control so I could go on with my day. I had never gone so far as to sell or pass what I took to anyone else, and I had never taken more than a handful of pills at a time. Still, this had gone on for two whole years.

"I have no idea how much I took, but I'm willing to set a dollar amount with you now and pay it down until I can pay it all off," I offer. As I finish my speech, the relief I feel mixes with a gnawing dread at how Frank might respond.

"Linda," he tells me, "I knew something was happening with you. I could see you had problems that were getting out of hand."

I wince as I reflect on my own lack of attention to my work back then, the many times I had showed up late or called in sick. I had been losing weight, too, and had a short fuse with co-workers due to the physical strain that addiction had been putting on my nervous system.

"But I'm really proud of you, Linda," Frank continued. "You have turned your life around."

His words feel like rain on a hot summer day. Could this man really forgive me so easily for something so horrible?

Frank goes on to say, "The way you have turned your life around is enough repayment for me." He does not expect me to pay him back, only to continue living clean and sober.

I leave the restaurant in a mild state of shock, hardly registering the friendly goodbyes of the staff as I step into the bright, sunlit afternoon. The pressure of seven years of worry has just lifted from my shoulders. I can hardly recognize myself without it.

I worked up the courage to make amends to my father at about five years sober, even though I knew I needed to do it from the very beginning. I waited this long because I had put so much focus on him and couldn't focus on my own character defects. I was unable to see my part, until now. His military grip on us—the way he had treated us all like his soldiers and his heavy drinking—it all had devastating consequences for everyone in the family. Still, after so much time in my recovery program and working with spiritual practices, I know that I can't do anything about his part of the equation. But what I *can* do is take responsibility for myself. I see clearly that I had contributed plenty to the negative tone of our relationship.

For one thing, I had enjoyed pushing his buttons. Even when I weighed less than 100 pounds, I had tried to fistfight my muscled Air Force dad, the drugs and alcohol inflating my courage and distorting my perspective. Instead of talking to him, I lashed out, using his poor behavior to justify my feelings and actions. I wanted my controlling father to feel out of control, just like I did. I was going to show him he couldn't control me, no matter how hard he tried.

When he had given me money while I was using, I took it without a second thought. I didn't care what giving it to me had cost him. He *owed* it to me. So I didn't think twice about lying to him about how I would use it (on more drugs, of course). He had hurt me, and now he was going to pay.

By the time I'm ready to make amends with Dad, my response to challenging relations is changing. My marriage with Jeff, easily one of the most positive things thus far in my life, still comes with its challenges. Jeff had grown up in a family faced with addiction, so I experience both of us dealing with the aftermath of these family patterns in our relationship. Working with these painful issues gives me compassion for the first time for what my parents had faced in their marriage. Before now, I had no understanding of what it took to stay in a relationship and work through challenges. Going to meetings of Adult Children of Alcoholics, I learn that partners let each other down so often because each is working through his or her own family-of-origin conditioning.

No longer at the age of 33 can I be a kid blaming my dad for all my problems.

Because I had taken the job in Belleville with the production company focused exclusively on making films to support recovery from drug and alcohol addiction, I'm now focusing my whole life on recovery and growth. And the deeper I go in this realm, the more I realize I no longer want to punish my father for events that happened in the past.

In fact, I don't want *either* of us to pay anymore. I now understand that I, and not he, lives caged in by my resentment, and I want freedom. Using the past to justify my resentments just doesn't fit anymore. I'm more interested in learning to see him for who he is now and to give him a chance to get to know who his daughter is without drugs and alcohol. These thoughts and feelings had controlled me much more viciously than my father ever had. I know I want to let all of that go and to release the shame of what I had done. I want *both* of us to be free.

But talking with my father about emotionally charged topics doesn't come easily. He already doesn't converse much, unless he's trying to teach me how to be more responsible. As a man who grew up during the Great Depression, he has very clear limits around what a man can and cannot say, especially on emotional subjects, even positive ones. Throughout my parents' marriage, I had never once heard him tell my mother he loved her. And I have never heard him say it to me, either.

So I begin to pray about how I can make amends with him. In meditation, I realize that my dad will never sit still long enough for me to have a conversation with him to make amends. So I decide to write him a letter.

The week before his birthday, I do just that. In my letter, I apologize for my behavior toward him when I had been drinking and drugging. I apologize for stealing money from him, for disrupting his marriage with my poor behavior, for not understanding the impact that my alcoholism at such a young age must have had on his personal and professional life, for what I put him through emotionally and physically, my disrespect, my anger and resentment. And the list goes on and on.

I also write that I'm sorry for using him to get money. I admit that I had manipulated him in this way, and I ask that he never give me money again. *I love you unconditionally*, I write, *and you don't need to buy my love anymore.*

With that off my chest and onto the stark white stationary, I seal the envelope, draw a heart where I had licked the flap and write "Poppo" on the front.

My father lives in O'Fallon, ten miles from where I work. On my hour lunch break, I have just enough time to get to his house to deliver my letter before I need to turn back around to return to work.

At his house, I step out of my car and up to the front porch, letter in hand. It seems so insubstantial, a plain white envelope marked with my father's nickname. How can something so small press so heavily on my insides? This little envelope carries the weight of a lifetime, of two lifetimes—mine and his.

I push it into the mailbox swiftly, no room for second-guessing myself. Today is my father's birthday, and this letter is my gift to him.

On the way home, I get a nudge to take a different route back to work than the one I had driven to get here. Following it, I turn onto Route 50. But pretty soon, I regret my decision. I find myself stuck at the end of a long line of cars in stop-and-go traffic. Road construction.

I don't have time for this. I need to be back at work! I must have misunderstood my intuition.

When I finally find myself at the front of the line, the person directing traffic turns the sign around to "Stop." *Damn*, I think. *Why me?* Then I look up, and a man is walking toward me.

My dad.

"Hi, Honey." After retiring from the military, he worked for the Labor Union. Today, he's working on the construction crew for this road and was briefly filling in for someone who had been directing traffic.

He leans in through my window, where out of the sunlight I can see his face more clearly. "How are you doing?"

At that, I give him a kiss. "Happy Birthday, Dad. I love you."

As we wait together for the signal for him to open up the flow of traffic and allow me to continue back to work, I make no mention of the letter waiting in his mailbox.

Lesson & Blessing

#10

Heal the Past.
Create a New Future.

My father and I have never spoken of the amends letter, even to this day. The only way I knew he had read it was that aside from a $50 gift each Christmas, he has never given me money. But the value of my choice to come clean with my father has been paying off ever since.

Every year I call my father on my A.A. birthday to tell him he can thank me for that number of years of a good night's sleep—a fun joke between us now, but one based on the real fears my parents once faced wondering during the dead of many nights if I was still alive.

I ended up carrying this motto with me for awhile: "Bring the body and the mind will follow." But I had to learn on my own that the mind didn't always follow quickly. Despite the new principles for living that the program was teaching me, I still struggled with self-judgment, doubt, and fear. My emotions often resembled the jagged teeth of a saw blade.

But the longer I stayed with the program and followed

the steps it outlined, the more I learned to work with these difficult emotions. Eventually, I realized the truth in what I had heard others say: I had a *thinking* problem long before I ever had a drinking or drug problem.

Addiction had arisen as the side effect of the way I looked at my life. Like so many others of my generation, I didn't trust the path the adults had given since they seemed so lost. But I also didn't have any alternate models for how to make good choices. In that vacuum, I let the pain of my childhood dictate my choices. By keeping that pain alive, I remained a child, expecting the world to take care of me.

Luckily, my program offered a different way of seeing and being in my life. Making amends with my father required me to forgive him for his part in the pain of my past. But it did more than this. In forgiving him, I learned to forgive myself.

Making amends with my father—and so many others—also taught me to take responsibility, not only for past actions, but also for how I lived in the present. Thanks to this process, I finally began growing up. When I began moving from resentment to forgiveness, it meant I needed to learn acceptance. Acceptance didn't mean I needed to like everything, but that whatever it is can be what it is.

When we're new in recovery, what we're primarily aware of is that we're flawed. Who we are now without alcohol and drugs, and who we have the capacity to become, feels like a big unknown in the beginning. So to cope with the fear of that big unknown, we hold onto our unworthiness. Letting go of that is like letting go of our identity.

While I was writing this book, I watched a video that illustrates the power of making amends. In it, more than 2,000 veterans went to Standing Rock Indian Reservation in South Dakota alongside Native Americans to protest the U.S. Government's policy changes around drilling on their sacred land. The simple fact that these veterans joined the Sioux Tribe and other protesters seemed significant to me, since I have a hard time imagining my own veteran father taking a stand like this.

These men did something even more significant, however. Down on one knee, each of them went before tribe elders to ask for forgiveness—not for something they had personally done, but for those crimes that previous veterans had perpetrated on the Sioux Tribe. In the ceremony, the leader from the veteran group spoke specifically of these wrongs.

"We broke treaties. We stole minerals from your land. We blasted the faces of our presidents onto your sacred mountain. Then we took still more away. We took your children. We tried to take your language ... your language that God gave you ... we polluted your Earth ... we hurt you in so many ways."

Then, as the speaker finished his speech, he knelt before the council of elders and said: *"We are at your service. We beg for your forgiveness."* [6]

As I watched this man speak, tears spilled down my face. One by one, each veteran knelt before the tribe elders to ask for forgiveness individually. How much courage must it have taken for these veterans to own the wrongs of ancestors? Did they personally "owe" the Sioux Tribe an apology for these wrongs? No. But this fact made the act even more powerful. Though they hadn't committed these crimes themselves, they had served in a system that had. This fact gave their apology special weight... and meaning.

As I watched this ceremony unfold, I was witnessing the essence of amends. Because of this act, some of the grief of this tribe could finally surface to be healed. I knew that the future, both for these men and for the tribe they had contacted, would unfold differently as a result.

When I began making amends in 1984, I didn't yet understand all this. I came at it back then like a Catholic girl with a dark past, hoping to gain favor with an angry God. I believed I was dealing with my own personal history. Now I know that when one makes amends, the healing goes all the

[6] YouTube, "Veterans Apologize To Sioux Tribe At Standing Rock Forgiveness Ceremony" (December 6, 2016)

way back through our ancestral lineage *and* creates a new future. Through the practice, we open new roads inside ourselves to greater understanding and deeper intimacy, both with ourselves and others. Because of this, we invent new destinies.

In my own journey, I came to the practice of making amends by way of desperately wanting freedom from drugs and alcohol. In time, though, I could see I wanted more than that. I wanted freedom, true freedom, from the inside out. Freedom from judgment, from anger, from resentment. I wanted freedom from fear, from shame. Whatever it took, I wanted to experience myself as free in every area of my life.

Thus, the path of recovery led me to the door of spirituality. Here, I would learn to cease fighting anyone or anything, including myself. My recovery program served as the foundation for all the future healing I would experience.

To this day, the blessings that I and others in my life have received from my commitment to amends remain too many to count. Among them, some of the most important are the deep lessons that I've learned that helped to create a new understanding of the way life really works: That when we hide from or resist the darkness that we've experienced, we can't see the Light. That the way home to our soul's essence is to see the Light where we think only this darkness lives. That the flawed parts also shape us and are part of our wholeness.

That through amends we create new possibilities...

Have you found a way to revisit your past shadows through a gentle lens? Through the lens of "that was supposed to happen." Or even, "Thank you, life, for that difficulty." Have you gotten to know both who you *are*, and who you *aren't*? What is your relationship with the challenges in your life?

The practices of looking both inwardly (inventory) and outwardly (amends) have the potential to transform *anyone* who takes them on earnestly, no matter the nature or size of past missteps.

Let the Walls Come Down

*"You find that being vulnerable
is the only way to allow your heart
to feel true pleasure that's so real it scares you."*
~ Bob Marley

" I just can't do it," I tell my brother. "I'm too exhausted."

For a minute, the line goes quiet. I grip the receiver tighter, waiting. Then, "Linda, you have to."

I cringe. For a month and a half now, I've been making a daily, 28-mile drive to the hospital to arrive at my mother's bedside by 9:00 a.m. Most of the time, I feel lucky to be able to do this. The year before, I had followed an instinct to quit my job as the

Substance Abuse Coordinator in St. Clair County to become an insurance agent, not even knowing why. Not long after, doctors discovered an inoperable cancerous tumor in my mother's brain. The breast cancer she had battled two years before had now metastasized, and along with the tumor, they eventually found lesions in her brain.

When I had received this news, I knew intellectually that she faced a serious health challenge. Then one day I watched as Mom had written me a check. All my life, she had the most beautiful hand-writing of anyone I knew. But the check in front of me looked as though it had been scrawled out by a young child. In an instant, I understood in my gut, what the doctors had actually meant with their careful euphemisms.

Mom didn't have much time left.

Fortunately, my career change meant that I could make my own hours, so I'm now free to be with her as much as possible as she makes her transition.

But that morning as my brother calls, I'm noticeably beginning to wear down. Dragging myself out of bed is harder and harder. The tiredness I feel starts to seep into the very marrow of my bones. I can't remember what life outside of the walls of a hospital room even feels like, and when I wake to three inches of a spring snow that morning, I feel ready to break.

Still, I can't let my brother down. He's working full-time and staying with Mom each evening in the hospice room, and I'm with her every day. From the dark rings under his eyes, I know he feels every bit as tired as I do.

With as much energy as I can muster, I slide into the ice cold driver's seat of my little Mazda RX7 and slowly back into the snow.

As I settle into Mom's room, I mechanically choose a tape of soothing music for her. Usually this rouses her. But instead of their usual brilliant blue, her eyes remain flat and gray today. This has been happening more frequently, and I know what it means. She's actively dying now, spending more and more time away from her body, her eyes going empty as her soul travels.

Frustration builds inside me as I notice it. Struggling with an obstinate tape recorder and my own bleary-eyed exhaustion, I finally lose it.

"Why am I doing this?!" I ask the limp frame in the bed beside me. She looks more like a skeleton than a person, muscles atrophied from weeks of paralysis from the neck down. Those flat eyes had sunk back into a skull now too large for its body. "You can't even tell me if the music is too loud, or if you want a different tape, or anything else for that matter. I don't even know if you're in there!"

With this, I sit and pray as I gaze out the window for five solid minutes asking for help. Then I look at my mother and it happens. Out of nowhere, her eyes light up, sky blue, and she winks at me. And just as swiftly, her eyes go flat. She's traveling again.

I feel like a bluebird has just flown through the room, leaving the echo of its song with me. All that time, my mother had been gathering her strength to deliver this message. She hasn't left yet. I'm not alone.

Warmth wells up in me, filling me with the strength to make it through another day in the hospital room.

Moments like this one, unmistakably magical, are beginning to add up for me, helping me to understand that even the difficult things I'm going through aren't happening *to* me but *for* me. Everything, no matter how uncomfortable, is ultimately adding up to my prayers being answered.

Another day, another miracle.

Of course, the real miracle with Mom had begun two years prior when I had finally decided to make amends with her. At a certain point in my process of making amends, I had reconciled with most everyone on my list—except Mom. Since the day she slapped me at age 12, I had been angry with her. Angry that she had hurt me that day, angry that she was so weak and needy and always looking for love, angry that she had been willing to ruin my life over a man. Most of all, I felt angry at myself for taking on her patterns of seeking love and approval from men to prove my own worth.

Mom had, and continued to, remind me of my own weakness. In my newfound clarity, I began to realize that she was reflecting to me the things I couldn't accept in either one of us. For most of our relationship, I had been using anger as my armor against it all. I had decided I needed a shield against a scary world, one where the person who was supposed to protect me and help me understand my life had instead blamed me and abandoned me to find my own way.

I had been angry at my mom for so long that I couldn't even imagine my life without that anger. How would I be safe without it? Another shield.

Mom's breast cancer diagnosis had changed the game. The doctor insisted at the time that the lump in her breast wasn't cancer, just a routine cyst that she needed to have removed. But on the afternoon of her surgery, I found my mother's husband, Jim, standing in the hallway at St. Elizabeth Hospital in tears. When he had collapsed into my arms, I knew what he couldn't yet speak out loud. The tumor was malignant.

Since then, a few days and a few recovery meetings had given me time to reflect on what was happening with Mom.

"I feel so afraid that I won't make amends with her before she leaves the planet," I had told my friend outside of the meeting we had both just attended. I could feel time slipping through my fingers as autumn's late afternoon light melted around us into dusk. "Why is it so hard for me to see my mom as another human being on her own learning journey, just like me? If I'm asking other people for forgiveness, why am I so unwilling to forgive her?"

"Can I pray with you about this, Linda?" my friend had asked. As he said it, I felt the world around us stop. Nothing else existed in that moment except for the two of us, lifted out of time and space. My friend, in his wisdom, was helping me to seek God to remove my shortcomings, just as our program taught.

Together, my friend and I had crawled into my little Mazda and asked God to give me the strength to have the willingness and openness to make amends with my mother. As we prayed together, I felt the world around me and within me rearrange itself. When we finished, my friend got out of the car, and I drove straight to the hospital.

When I arrived, Mom's room was crammed with people. Family and close friends chattered in clumps around the room. To me, the noise seemed louder than it probably was, simply because I felt so vulnerable after my prayers with my friend. But as I walked closer to Mom, the crowd began to disperse. Without any effort from me, the room gradually cleared, until only Mom and I remained.

Gingerly, I walked to the edge of Mom's bed and sat beside her. Without any small talk, I launched into the speech I had been rehearsing the whole drive there.

"Mom, I'm so afraid that you're going to die before I'm able to tell you that I love you."

By now, Mom was a few days past the surgery. Her color is back, along with her light, loving spirit. I had her full attention.

"I realize now that when I was a little girl, 12 years old, and you had that affair, then you slapped me across the face for talking back to you, right then I walled you out." Words were pouring out of me, words I had held for most of my life. "Mom, when I walled you out, I walled out all the bad *and* all the good in our relationship. And I've never given you the chance to be forgiven or to forgive."

With this, I crawled into the bed to lie next to her. "Mom, I walled out all the good with all the bad," I repeated. "I cut out all the joy from our lives. I want to change that. Will you forgive me?"

Tears streamed down our faces. We held each other and cried.

I left Mom's room that night a different person. I'd found the courage to allow a power much greater than my own to move through me. I knew in that moment that the transformation this moment had sparked would come to affect every part of my life.

It also affected Mom, more dramatically than I could imagine. Shortly after she got home from the hospital, I found myself in her living room with my friend Jane. The two of us watched as Mom poured a whiskey highball.

"Well, this is my last drink," she announced suddenly.

Flabbergasted, I stuttered out some kind of question: "What do you mean?"

"I know I have a problem with alcohol. It's time for me to get some help."

Nothing could have surprised me more. Not once had I ever said a word to Mom about her relationship to alcohol or drinking, which I'd noticed begin to get out of control in her second marriage. She'd been watching me move through the process of recovery for more than eight years, but had never asked me any questions about it or expressed any interest in attending a meeting. Something about our tender moment in the hospital, together with a near-death experience must have dislodged something in her. She now wanted to make the most of the time she still had.

I realized that the grace I had received that evening in prayer had affected my mother as much as it had me. The universe had been ready, waiting to pour this blessing into both of us. I simply needed to take the first step.

After a moment's pause, I responded to Mom's request brightly. "I can't help you, Mom. But she can!" With this, I pointed to my friend Jane. By then, I knew better than to try to help my own mother with recovery.

Jane took Mom to her first meeting and became my mom's sponsor. And for the first time in her life, at age 57, Mom began to face the ways that alcohol had impacted her life.

She had taken on recovery with a passion. Even though the self-help movement had come from *my* generation, for the first time Mom began to question all the models and ideals *she* had swallowed in her upbringing. Before, she had always played the obedient wife, letting others think for her. But after embracing recovery, she began waking up. With her sponsor, she could finally share things she had bottled up her whole life. Supported by others who had also lived with an alcoholic parent, she saw her own history with fresh eyes.

As Mom was waking up, I, too, started waking up. I began to see that her codependent behavior, things like crying and begging, which I had always seen as childish, actually came with the territory of a childhood like hers. Many who had grown up with an alcoholic parent had learned behaviors that often created the inability to be emotionally present to others. I also began to understand that she had been unavailable to me because she suffered so much pain. It had made her unavailable to herself, to life.

For the first time, we began having real conversations as we unwound the history between us. As I watched Mom heal her own patterns, the part of me that had grown up as the daughter of an alcoholic father, constantly needing love and approval from men, began to heal as well.

And our relationship blossomed. In some ways, we did many of the same things we always had, like cooking or baking together. Mom loved coming to visit the house Jeff and I had built in the country, where she could relax and enjoy the beauty. And over time, we had so much more to talk about than recipes, magazines, or the weather. Because both of us *wanted* to spend time together, we added fun, new activities to our repertoire, such as taking a class in wildflower design.

I watched the prayer of my heart come true as Mom became a real person to me, sharing her fears and dreams, the mistakes she had made, her hopes for the future. I became real to her, too. She stopped comparing me to other people—my brother, his former fiancé, my cousin, someone on TV—and began to accept and appreciate me, as is. Almost overnight, the chore of spending time with Mom as the dutiful daughter had become a pleasure.

So when the diagnosis had come, the second diagnosis, of a tumor not in Mom's breast but now in her brain, with cancer spreading throughout her body, I felt ready in one sense. After all, I had made amends, and our relationship had healed in ways I never could have dreamed. If she left the planet tomorrow, my conscience would be clear.

But the fact that we had grown so close, so quickly, made this news excruciating. I wasn't ready to lose Mom. I had only just gotten her back, after a lifetime of being separated from her. The time I have left with her is more precious than ever.

The next many months of my life I focused exclusively on Mom, taking her to and from wearying doctor appointments far from her home. On our long drives together, I began opening up to her even more. I wanted my mom to know me. I shared my spiritual beliefs with her, things like my understanding that our souls come here to have an experience of life on Earth, and that we continue as souls even after we leave the body.

"Do you think you could come and see me after you die?" I asked. "Yes," she replied, "my own mother came to see me after crossing over and has been nearby ever since."

This conversation trembled with tenderness. We held hands as I drove. In this strange place between life and death, the veil between mother and daughter was lifted. We rode together as two souls traveling through the world together, learning from and teaching each other. Only then did I begin to realize that our journey together would not end with Mom's death.

One day after a doctor's appointment, Mom said, "I want to take you somewhere." Without revealing where we were headed, she directed me left, right, straight. When I parked the car, we had arrived at the cemetery where she would be buried.

Delicately, she began to explain what she wanted for her memorial as she knew it would be difficult for Ron, Jim, and me to make all those decisions on our own, with the pressure of grief and family responsibility weighing on all of us. So she had hoped to make things easier this way.

She was preparing me for her death.

As Mom's condition worsened, she ended up in the hospital and eventually on hospice care. But a shortage of nurses, not just in our hospital but in the whole region, meant we needed to be with her as much as possible. Daily I watched Mom waste away, eventually becoming paralyzed from the neck down.

Now, my turn has come to muster courage.

On Valentine's Day, my father, who had long since remarried, walks into Mom's hospital room with his current wife, Pat, and a dozen long-stemmed yellow roses. By then, Mom can't speak properly, her words often disjointed and out of sync. Yet that night she speaks clearly. Their last words to each other are: "I love you."

This has a powerful effect on me. Because of the forgiveness I had offered them, my whole family had entered their own form of recovery. Like me, they are growing. Forgiving. With all the insanity we had endured together, we now have all the joy, too.

The night of my eighth anniversary with Jeff, I find myself not with him, but with my cousin who's visiting St. Louis. On my way home, I stop at the hospital where the nurses let me into Mom's room.

In that bed, a skeleton looks back at me. More than a month and a half had passed this way, with Mom immobilized from the inoperable tumors. Something about that night, seeing her this way...

somehow I know she won't live to see the next day.

"Mom, I love you," I tell the figure on the bed. "It's okay to go now. It's okay. I want to say goodbye."

On the way to the hospital the next morning, I take a curve on a road just outside of Freeburg, Illinois. As I round the corner, a strange, dizzying sense of dislocation washes over me. I look at the clock in the car and the time is 9:15. It feels as if the energy of the planet itself has just shifted underneath me, as though the world is no longer spinning on its axis in the same way.

When I arrived at the hospital, I learned that at exactly 9:15, Mom had died.

Lesson & Blessing
#11

Reweaving the Fabric of Reality

In the short time Mom and I had spent together after I made amends, I had rewritten my past. No longer did I feel like an angry girl, alone and adrift in a scary world with no one to protect me. I had become a child beloved of her mother. At one point, Mom even told me that I had become a better daughter and woman than she ever imagined was possible.

Moments like this astonished me. Brick by brick, I'd been dismantling the wall I built against Mom in childhood. Once she left, whatever remained of that wall turned to dust. It blew away completely.

Like a lot where an old house has been torn down, I now had an open space inside me. That space scared me, but it also called to me like a blank canvas. I clearly saw my power to create my own life. After all, I had made the choices that kept my mother and me apart for so long. Pointing a finger at her, blaming her for the ways she failed as a mother, insisting she had to make things work between us—all of that had accomplished nothing. But in one courageous moment, when I admitted to her what I had done to keep us separate, I had reshaped both our past and our future. By taking responsibility for our relationship, I had taken control of my destiny.

I remember when I took up the study of painting months after Mom had passed. I sat down one evening with canvas, brushes, and the intent to paint with my mother in mind. As I often had, I parked myself in the overstuffed armchair in the living room, looking out the west window at the sunset while I reflected on what to paint.

Love swept through me, pushing me like a wave from the armchair and into my bedroom. I took to my knees, and prayed for God to help me understand. *What do I do with all this love for a person who's no longer here?* I had finally broken through all the veils of anger, resentment, and blame, yet I was only 36 and had already lost my mother. And I had walled her out for nearly 24 years because I had thought it was easier not to feel the pain.

Out of nowhere, a passion for Mom, for our connection and our experience together, overtook me. Emotion ripped through me so intensely that I couldn't pick up a brush. I was afraid that if I painted what I felt, because the passion was so big, that I would go insane.

As these feelings washed over me, I realized in amazement that there was actually love tied to the moment she had slapped me. Even then—especially then—I loved her. The instance in which I experienced that intense level of difficulty and pain had made our later journey from anger to tenderness, from judgment to understanding, all the more precious to me. When my mother had slapped me, it felt like the beginning of the end. Now I know that it's what opened every door afterward.

The feeling engulfed me. I couldn't paint it, couldn't express the depth of the love between us. I realized that it wasn't too late to experience this love, and that it was now with me forever.

At that time, I couldn't explain to anyone the connection this love bore to pain. But now I can. Have you ever loved without any pain? I saw that we can seldom have one without the other. If my wall against my mother had protected me from pain, it had also kept out this love, this joy. The opposites coexisted, two sides of the same coin.

No longer would I sacrifice this experience of love for the sake of keeping myself safe. If pain came with love, I wanted to feel it. Through Mom's death, I was learning how to embrace both halves of the equation.

In my heart that night, kneeling by the bed, I was saying to Mom, "If I knew before what we would go through together, I would do it all over again. The blessing of knowing you is more precious than any pain I have endured."

The biggest blessing of this time was finally getting to have an authentic, meaningful relationship with Mom. More than once, she shared with me that the last years of her life, which she had dedicated to sobriety, personal growth, and understanding herself, were her happiest. Looking back, I'm in awe at the act of love she offered me toward the end of her life, preparing me for her death. She was only 59 years old, yet she faced death with such courage. She used her strength to prepare everyone around her for *their* journey through the experience, not just her own.

Following the step of amends allowed me to reap significant rewards—finally having an intimate relationship with my mother. In addition, watching my family members engage their own healing journeys became one of the greatest blessings of my life, which continues to this day with my deepening relationships with my brother Ron and Dad. Together, we've rewoven our family tapestry to include everything that we experienced, and we've made it whole.

I continually remind myself of the importance of our humanity. Our parents had their own life experiences and wounding before they ever touched or raised us. Mom wasn't doing anything *to* me, rather she was responding to the emotionally overwhelming experiences of her past, just as I was to mine.

Many of us, when we experience pain, want to shut it out, avoid it, and make sure it doesn't ever happen again. Now I know that *every* experience in life has something to teach us, to grow us, to make us more whole. I no longer shut out the painful experiences, but rather embrace them as part of the path.

Remember that discomfort has a message. You won't know what miracles are available unless you open the door to the present rather than live as if your past is running the show. Part of this includes exploring, and then releasing, the stories you have about others—*especially* your parents. You'll begin to see more clearly that your challenging experiences aren't only about you. Your recovery, in whatever form it takes, isn't only a blessing to you, but all those around you.

Coming Home to Myself

"It was when I stopped searching for home within others and lifted the foundations of home within myself I found there were no roots more intimate than those between a mind and body that have decided to be whole."

~ Rupi Kaur

The day of Mom's funeral I wake up at 2:30 a.m., startled out of a dream. I had seen Mom.

"I told you I would come to you when I crossed over," she said, her body—her pre-cancer body, slender and strong—as vivid and real to me in that state as it had been before her illness. Our conversations about life after death seep into my mind and bring me solace in the startle.

"But Linda, I know you won't believe it's actually me coming to you, and not just a dream, unless you have proof."

Of course, she's right.

She continues, "Check with Jim. He went into the safety deposit box yesterday. There is a document in it—the closing of my mother's estate. It has a date on it that will prove to you that you're not just having a dream. I really did come to see you. That date will also show you that my own mother helped me cross over."

Mom had married Jim many years before. I ache to call him right away, but I know I shouldn't at this hour. Instead, I install myself on the living room couch with a mug of herbal tea, waiting for the moment when I can call. Staring through the large living room windows, into the sprawling lawn and forest in front of the house, I mull over the day ahead of me. On the clock, I have just a few short hours before I'll find myself at Mom's memorial service. But that time seems like days stretching out in front of me. Grief forces everything into slow motion.

Never again will I exchange a recipe with her, pick up the phone to tell her a funny story, or hear about what she had learned in recovery. Living without her feels like conducting a symphony missing one instrument. How will I ever recalibrate the song of my life without her notes?

But I'm also grieving a past that will never be. Despite my adult understanding of its impossibility, the little girl inside still wishes for the perfect childhood, the picket fence, the happy family. I feel deep sorrow, not just for the mother my mom never was, but also for the daughter I might have been.

The future and the past twist up inside me—a knot I can't untie.

What can I do with all this pain? I no longer have the option to kill it with alcohol or drugs.

Dozing in and out of consciousness, I watch the light come into the day. With it, I move in and out of waves of emotion. A huge wave of sorrow sweeps over me, then crashes. I have a moment of rest, then smaller waves of pain break and swirl around me. Then bigger ones again, rising, tugging my feet from underneath me. I am only 36 years old. Life has just started to happen for me. I want to rewind, back to the time when Mom and I could still sit on my living room couch to watch the sunrise together.

But I know I can't go back, only forward—without Mom, the woman I had only just begun to know.

There's nowhere to turn except to sit with the emotional pain. I call my sponsor. I talk it over with Jeff when he wakes up. And I continue to sit.

Finally it's late enough in the morning that I can make the call.

"I'll call you right back," my brother promises. Ron had stayed the night at Jim's house and had answered Jim's phone. His voice over the line seems unreal, more a memory than something actually happening. After hearing the story of my dream, he had agreed to find out if Jim knew anything about a document from the closing of our grandmother's estate.

After what feels like an endless wait, I pick up the phone on the first ring. My brother has the document in hand. Indeed, Jim had retrieved it from the safety deposit box the day before. My brother scanned it for a date.

"Ah, here it is. It's when Grandmother died. March 14, 1957."

Chills shoot up and down my spine. My own mother had just passed on March 14, 1989. What's more, she had died the same way her own mother had, the one-two punch of breast and brain cancer. Later at the wake, I learned from half a dozen people who had known Mom through work or social circles that she believed for many years that she would die the same way that her own mother had. But she had never confessed this to me. Only the dream had pointed me to this aspect of Mom's death.

This dream had momentarily relieved the pain of grief by giving me one last moment with her. Still dazed with grief, though, I didn't fully understand what had happened. It was no standard dream. Mom had actually visited me from the other side.

About six weeks later, I awake once again from a dream at 2:30 a.m. Like before, I had seen Mom. This time, I know I'm not merely imagining this encounter.

Not too long before this, Jim had asked me to come over to clean out Mom's closet. He couldn't handle smelling her in the bedroom and had wanted all her clothes removed.

But in the dream, Mom says to expect trouble with Jim when

I go to the house. It doesn't surprise me to hear her say it. Jim had been an excellent partner to my mother, but I had a more complex relationship with him. The pain of old experiences still lingers, and Jim had made it clear to me before Mom passed that neither my brother nor I would get any of Mom's money as he wouldn't allow her to create a will.

I had reassured her then, "It's okay, Mom. Don't hurt yourself over this. More than anything else, I have my time with you. That's what matters. I have your love." But in one conversation with Jim present, Mom had said very clearly, "I want my kids to have the mementos that were mine with their dad." None of the things she talked about—a tea set from Japan, a musical Japanese lamp, keepsakes from Japan and Germany, a few family heirlooms—are particularly valuable. But they mean a lot to my brother and me.

In the dream, Mom warns me that Jim will have trouble letting go of these things that had belonged to her and my father. But I shouldn't worry about this, she explains, because Laura, Jim's daughter, will come over while I'm still going through the closet. She'll mitigate the conflict so that Jim can let go.

That morning, I went to their house as we had planned, without giving too much thought to the visit. While I'm cleaning, Laura shows up to help me. In the midst of our piles, I ask Jim when I can have the things that had belonged to my mom and dad together. This question upsets him, and he refuses to let me have anything.

Then Laura steps in explaining how the children of his wife need something sentimental to remind them of their mother. With this,

Jim relents and I go home with the few precious items Mom had left for my brother and me.

Once again, my dream and waking world have lined up. I now know that Mom really *had* been reaching out to me. These dreams become a confirmation of the world that exists beyond what I can perceive with my eyes alone. Before Mom died, I believed in reincarnation. Now I'm receiving direct messages to prove that she and I remain connected in spirit.

Mom's death also teaches me the value of her life. Without her physically present, I can appreciate the many facets of her personality and life experience in a way I couldn't while she remained. Now I'm able to experience life itself with a kind of reverence I had only understood intellectually before Mom passed.

Cherishing Mom's life after she dies sparks something in me. I can now see a bigger picture than I ever had. Whatever I begin doing with passing moments might seem small. And on one level, each one really is; no past or future actually exists beyond them. But over time, these passing moments of "small" experiences had added up to the sum of my whole life.

I now know that I want to create my life from the place of magic and healing that I had discovered with Mom.

This vantage point had never occurred to me before this moment. Facing my own mortality feels like standing at the top of a mountain looking down for the first time at a city where I've always lived. From here, I can see the places where paths and roads converge, the structures that surround me, and the way those thought-structures are both shaping and limiting my perspective. The details of my life begin fitting into one coherent whole that had previously seemed like puzzle pieces that didn't fit together.

At one point in her later years, my mother had brought her father to Illinois to live with her and mend their relationship. Recalling their profound healing process, I'm inspired to begin to look more deeply at the relationships with the men in *my* life.

In looking more closely, I realize how much I had needed Jeff to love me in order to make me feel like I mattered. Like Mom had with her husband (my father), I, too, had entered my marriage as the shell of a person, not knowing myself or how to make my own choices. Jeff had become my North Star. Especially in the early days, my course had always been set by his—his interests, his desires, his ideas. As I understood and forgave Mom for her behavior toward my father, I admit to myself that I'm repeating some of the same patterns.

Like dominoes falling, this knocks over the way I relate with Jeff. Who am I, apart from him? Before Mom died, I probably couldn't have even understood the question. But my own dreams are emerging, pushing up against my limits the way a dormant seed bursts from dark, rich soil.

One Saturday morning, I wake up holding Jeff. I am returning from a deep sleep, where I was dreaming... something. What?

Gradually an awareness is coming. Something about Jeff and me.

Oh, right. Jeff and me. Images from the dream resurface. We had been brother and sister, except in the dream we had both looked differently. It feels like a memory more than a dream, but from another lifetime.

As the dream-memories come back to me in that barely awake state, I begin to admit to myself something that has been dawning on me gradually for a while.

For most of our relationship, I had lived inside of Jeff's life dreams. Like a house on a distant horizon, my own hopes and desires had been hovering at the edges of my consciousness. With Mom's passing, though, I suddenly arrive at that once faraway place. Up close, I can see my own dreams more clearly.

Some of them still match my life in the woods with Jeff. But most don't. I want to travel, to expand my studies, to build a career, something I don't know how to do easily with our rural, back-to-the-land lifestyle. But most of all, I want to know God and to know myself. *Why am I here? How do we heal?*

In many ways, I'm yearning for something I still cannot name. But it's calling to me just the same.

Of course, Jeff is naturally a spiritual person, following The Golden Rule and living a healthy life. But he has no interest in discussing the spiritual topics that tug at my curiosity. As much as I want to stay with him, I know that if I stay, I'll never be able to truly pursue what I care about most.

Gradually, almost imperceptibly, we'd been growing apart. It wasn't a sign that either one of us had done something wrong—only that our time together had served its purpose, taking both of us closer to our own hearts' desires.

That Saturday morning as I woke from my dream about a life when Jeff and I had been brother and sister, I finally admit to myself what I had already felt coming: Jeff and I have completed our work together. We've learned what we needed to learn. My heart is nudging me to go.

One part of me hates this. I had married a man who was so good and so kind that plenty of women would have loved to stand in my place. Besides, a good Catholic girl can't leave her husband. Who do I think I am, walking away from such a great life? How can I even consider hurting Jeff, who has given me so much? Without him, I'm not sure I would have ever come so far in my own growth and healing.

On the other hand, I had learned in my time with Mom that a healthy relationship, the kind I know I want to be in, wouldn't require either person to sacrifice his or her own dreams.

For a while, the good Catholic girl inside me goes to war with the authentic self I'm becoming. But eventually, I can't deny that another future is pulling me to itself. Over the years of our marriage, I had begun frequenting metaphysical bookstores, seeing holistic doctors, doing cleanses, and scheduling massages. I read about quantum physics, about the power of thought in books like James Allen's "As A Man Thinketh," and countless books and articles about recovery and healing. I had deepened my studies of Eckankar and anything else that would expand my spiritual borders. But instead of finding my curiosity satisfied, I only felt hungry for more. Just as Jeff's dream of building a house had become a passion that shaped our whole lives, I had awoken the fires of a passion so hungry for spiritual growth, it demanded everything I had.

The next thing I know, the good Catholic girl caves. I ask Jeff for a divorce.

Even in the midst of the process of separation and divorce, I struggle to understand why I am making this decision. My father rails against me for walking away with only $10,000 and a car. "Why aren't you taking half of the assets, the portion that is rightfully yours?" Dad asks. "Are you doing this out of some kind of guilt for leaving the man?"

I explain to him what I know is true. In our time together, Jeff had given me more than I could ever repay. And if I ask for half of what we have, I know Jeff will need to sell the house. I don't want to take that dream from him any more than I want to give him half of mine which doesn't have a price tag.

On a late winter's day in 1990, Jeff and I part paths.

As I drive away, I don't look back. I can't. Even though I'm leaving, I feel more love for Jeff in that moment than I ever had before.

Lesson & Blessing

#12

Dream Life

When I moved alone into a cute, downtown apartment, remodeled with vaulted ceilings and big windows, I did so with a strange mixture of grief and anticipation. On the one hand, I was suffering from the loss of both my mom and my husband, Jeff, who had supported me in countless ways for many years. On the other hand, I faced the opportunity to pursue my own biggest dreams.

Grief is the most important emotion that most people don't know how to deal with. Why? When we have grief come up, it's often complicated by previous life experiences that haven't yet been fully grieved and processed. For me, to begin pursuing these dreams required that I felt the grief and allowed it to move through me.

At the time, I kept trying to figure it all out with my mind. How could I love someone this much but not choose to be with him? Where would my decision to strike out on my own take me? I couldn't make sense of what I had done.

But nothing about this process followed logic. I would

never understand it with my mind. I was *feeling* my way into it with my body the way someone might find the path through a dark cave by edging along its wall, each next step carefully tested. More than once, I found myself on the carpet, on my knees in prayer. I was going on blind faith, and I needed help.

One evening during that time, I was coming home from my girlfriend Jane's house when I happened to glance across 17th Street. Unexpectedly, I saw Jeff. He was walking into a house I didn't know, with a woman I didn't know—a pregnant woman.

I watched as he helped her gingerly up to the front door. We hadn't yet completed our divorce. But at that moment, I understood. He had moved on.

The knowledge of it had hit me like a gale force wind. Never mind that I had initiated this process. It hurt to see Jeff with another woman. Still, I could also see another aspect of the situation. I understood that something more had become possible for Jeff through our parting, a future I couldn't have given him, but one he was meant to fulfill. I had never gotten pregnant with him, and we had never made plans to have children.

A jumbled mixture of relief and sorrow washed through me as I watched Jeff step into the pregnant woman's home.

I didn't feel angry or resentful. I didn't ask: *Why wasn't it me?* I understood something in my emotions and body that I couldn't put into words. Through silent tears, I admitted to myself that something bigger was going on in the process of our separation. I had lived like I was supposed to make my life look a certain way—all those values of my childhood, my upbringing that told me I shouldn't get a divorce. But I had never considered that my decision, prompted by an inner knowing, could also be about someone else's life—Jeff's—and how it needed to unfold. I realized that Spirit had a plan for him, one I did not fit into any longer. I had spent eight years building a house with Jeff. Now I was learning how to come home to myself.

Divorce in our culture often tells us that somebody has to be wrong in order for someone else to be right. I didn't need to find a reason why life wasn't good enough, rather following my dreams was enough. It allowed Jeff and me to walk into more authentic lives that we were each growing into. And we're always growing. I received the blessing of being shown that love comes in many forms.

Sometimes the lessons and blessings of our lives weave so tightly together that we can't separate one from the other—the lesson of facing grief courageously and feeling it fully allows the blessing of expansion and new possibilities to arise on the other side of it. And the lessons don't come in one big swoop. We live into them, moment by moment, and through this we uncover the blessings.

This time also taught me the importance of listening to my inner whispers. It allowed me to receive essential messages through dreams, as strange as it may have seemed. I learned how to have an open mind and receive what life had to offer in all its forms. I learned to trust more than just my logical mind, but to include what my body and emotions had to say as well.

You may wonder if you can trust yourself—listening to that still, small voice inside. It doesn't shout. It doesn't show the next unfoldment or next step. It lives in that pregnant space between hope and faith.

The Winding Road

"For every moment of joy. Every hour of fear.
For every winding road that brought me here.
For every breath, for every day of living.
This is my Thanksgiving"
~Don Henley

"Something has just happened around the moon in your chart, something important. Is it possible that a mother figure recently passed away?"

The silver-haired woman across the dining room table had been practicing astrology for decades. Dressed in a plain white blouse, black slacks, and a stylish necklace, she greets me at the door of her tidy, spacious home with a down-to-earth presence that puts me at ease.

I'd come here tentatively, on a recommendation—my first time to visit an astrologer, and I hadn't known what to expect. But I could have met this woman in a business meeting. Almost immediately, she gains my respect.

But now, with these opening words about my mother, she also has my attention. At 36, I feel devastated by so many recent losses. The few short years of friendship I had experienced with Mom after making amends with her had changed my life. Now I don't know how to go on without her. To make matters worse, I can no longer turn to Jeff for solace and support. My life is now unmoored.

The grief I still struggle with over these losses, especially the loss of Mom, spurs me to leave my comfort zone to set up this unusual appointment. I hadn't said a word about any of this to the astrologer, though. How can she know something so personal about me?

She goes on, "In 1973," she says, "it looks as though you could have left the planet." Indeed, I had left the planet, at least for awhile. That was the year of my second suicide attempt, then agreed to return to my body with the *Presence's*—which I'd since come to know and name as *Spirit*—assurance that my life would get better. Since then, my life *has* gotten better.

Though my life is getting better, most days still feel like an uphill climb. I'm 10 years clean, and so much emotional energy continues to arise. I'm learning to feel my emotions, and at times they are so acute I don't know fully how to deal with them. They're jagged and seem to be out of proportion to the actual events that are happening.

The astrologer continues pointing out past highlights of my life with a degree of accuracy that astonishes me. She talks about the strain of my life, the way I always grappled to find balance. "It looks like you've often wanted to give up."

She continues, "You came in as an old soul, to heal your past karma. And you've been doing a good job of it. If you can just hold on until 40, your life is going to turn around."

Hold on until 40?! Well, I've been holding on for 36 years now. What was four more? I imagine myself at the end of a long rope, with an abyss underneath me. Now, I'm tying a knot around my hand with the last of the rope. I can hold on. I will hold on.

I feel like a voice is speaking to me again like that one in the hospital. "Your life will get better," it had said to me then, and offered me the choice to live. Now this astrologer says it with different words: "Your life is going to turn around." Now I have a new opportunity: To trust the inner guidance that I'm receiving and to take more steps into the unknown future.

Over the coming years, I turn this reading over in my mind like rubbing a worry stone. Would it come true? I have no idea. But I certainly hope it will. After all, I tell myself, she had nailed the details on so many other things. Still, her promise seems elusive.

"Thank you, Delta Airlines," I intone under my breath, clicking the seatbelt over my waist. In a matter of minutes, the plane I had just boarded is leaving the tarmac. I feel more than a little nervous about what awaits me when it lands.

For a while now, I had been searching for work. Since the insurance job I had taken during Mom's passing only paid on commission, I needed to find something more stable. I was looking for something steady with benefits.

When I saw the advertisement for a position as a flight attendant in the newspaper, I felt myself perk up a little. Travel, service—I liked the idea. But was I really flight attendant material? When I found myself at an interview for the job in St. Louis, I was still wondering. The questions they asked for this entry-level position made me think they had no interest in hiring me.

"Oh well," I told myself as I left the interview. "At least I tried." Chalk one up to experience.

Not long after, a girlfriend of mine who lives in Georgia called.

"We're hosting a reception of sobriety," she told me. This common celebration in my recovery program recognizes people who have remained sober for many years. They wanted to include me in the celebration as I had been her sponsor, and she would be recognized for a number of years of sobriety.

The invitation came at a moment when I had been feeling shaky, at loose ends. I knew I had made the right decision to leave Jeff, yet I was concerned about finances and I didn't have a solid job, and the trip to Georgia would be costly. The reception, though, seemed like the perfect way to anchor me to the many blessings I still had in my life. There I would be with a dear friend I had known for many years, and we would mark her sobriety anniversary, a milestone as precious as any I had celebrated. I felt flattered at the invitation and hoped I could attend.

Another thing about this invitation tugged at me. I had such a powerful connection to Georgia from my own childhood. The idea of visiting Warner Robins, my old hometown, filled me with anticipation. Since my family's hasty exit just after my father had returned from Thailand when I was 12, I hadn't been back. How would it look to me, what would I feel after all this time?

Of course, I wasn't kidding myself. I knew that my current financial situation would ultimately decide whether or not I could go to Georgia.

"I would love to do it," I told my friend. "Give me a few days to see if I can make it work."

When I ran the numbers, though, I got the answer I had feared. Since I had left Jeff, my budget had gotten tight. I just didn't have the money to make the flight. I would have to call my friend and decline.

As soon as I got settled into my apartment after a long day of errands and job hunting, I intended to do just that. On the way in, I grabbed the mail. As I sorted it, I noticed a letter from Delta. Instead of the polite rejection letter I had expected, however, I found a round-trip ticket in the envelope to attend a second round of interviews—in Atlanta, Georgia. The ticket would let me stay in the area for up to two weeks before making the flight back home.

Just moments before I had thrown away the slip of paper scrawled with numbers which I thought had sealed my fate, closing the door on attending the reception and visiting Warner Robins again. In an instant, all that had changed. The flight with Delta for an interview would put me there at the perfect time! Not only would I be able to make the reception, I might even get a job out of the whole thing. Without a doubt, I knew this had come as a gift from Spirit.

The sight of Sacred Heart Catholic School in Warner Robins rattles me at first. Even though I hadn't set eyes on the place since age 12, nothing but the library had changed. As I stand in the parking lot, staring at the place in surprise, I watch one of my friends from the eighth grade drive into the roundabout. I recognize her instantly because, to me, she looks exactly the same as when we had attended the school together so many years before. She's coming to pick up her own kids who now attend this school.

Have I entered the twilight zone? How can all these little details be falling into place with so little effort on my part? Even though I had experienced serendipity plenty of times in my life by this point, each time it takes me by surprise.

As I walk the somber, echoing halls, I feel like Alice in Wonderland falling through a jumbled kaleidoscope of old memories and emotions. Seeing my childhood friend, together with her young daughter, reminds me of how much I had loved this place. After all, this school had given me my first sense of belonging in a chaotic, transient life. Perhaps I recognize my friend so easily because she had meant so much to me those many years ago.

On the other hand, my love for this place had ended in pain. I had been expelled, not for my own bad behavior, but my mother's. Abruptly, I had been torn away from all that I cared about, with no say in the matter. In time, this event had taken on epic proportions in my own mind. Through the years of addiction, I had turned to the story over and over to prove to myself the unfairness of my life and how terribly my mother had treated me.

Then Mom and I had reconciled. I had forgiven her for the mistakes she had made. But had I fully forgiven myself? Before we reconnected, I had used the story of Mom's mistakes here in Warner Robins to keep her away from me for so long. Now, I would never get back all those lost years with a woman whom had become my friend. Why had I spent so much time separating myself from her?

I wince as I realize how much my pride had cost.

As I walk through these familiar halls, I'm discovering something else, too. All these years, I had been carrying around a tight, fiery ball of rage against the nun who had expelled me. How dare she treat a child this way? With one harsh decision, she had shattered my sense of self and wrecked my relationship with God. She hadn't even had the decency to explain any of it to me.

As these feelings flare up in me, my mind falls back to the reception of sobriety which I had just attended a few days before. In my purse, I find my own sobriety coin and begin to fumble with it. In my program, I had agreed to make "a searching and fearless moral inventory" of myself, not just once, but as a lifestyle. I'd promised, to myself and to many others, to make direct amends to anyone I'd harmed, whenever possible. Even more than an exercise in staying alcohol- and drug-free, my years of sobriety had become a commitment to a way of life and practices. Yet what does this token mean if I won't live the principles it represents?

So for the first time, I get honest with myself about this nun. Had she made a mistake? To me, it sure looked like it. Could I do anything about that now? Not a thing. And what about me? Maybe I hadn't done anything back then to deserve her punishment. Yet I've been harboring resentment nearly every day since. I begin to think that this is also a mistake, which has me question hers.

A part of me doesn't want to let this resentment go. How can I keep myself safe from future hurt without it? By now, however, I'd done enough work in recovery to recognize, at least mentally, that the angry, blaming attitude I'm holding toward the Sister is actually hurting, not protecting, me. I had learned this lesson loud and clear with Mom: Owning my part in the past events, no matter what another person had done, gives me the swiftest release from it.

Once again, I need to make amends for my own attitudes, feelings, thoughts, and actions. Not for the nun. For me.

At the school's front desk, I ask for the nun's address. Before I leave the building, I begin composing in my head the letter that would become my amends to the Sister. In this letter, I would explain that I'd once been addicted to alcohol and drugs, but that I'd been in recovery for many years now. My recovery program had taught me the importance of making amends for past wrongs. I'm writing to her now to make amends for the anger and resentment I'd held toward her all this time for her choice to expel me from the school. As a clean and sober adult now, I recognize that the adults around me at the time were simply making the best decisions they could. I would conclude the letter by asking for the nun's forgiveness for so many years of anger toward her.

Months later, I receive a reply to the letter I'd sent that I'd begun composing mentally that day in Georgia. The nun's response, if a little formal, also conveys a tone of warmth. She appreciated receiving my letter, she explains, and she's happy that I had found recovery and taken a positive path in my life. Then she confesses, as gracefully as possible, that she honestly doesn't remember me or my expulsion.

I laugh out loud. I had allowed that moment with this nun to define so much of my identity! Yet she had registered little more than a blip on her internal radar from our encounter, a moment so business-as-usual that she can't even recall it happening.

Her letter puts things into perspective for me. Before, the pain I had been lugging around seemed so important, so unique; yet only I had suffered so horribly. Now, my version of the story just looks like garden-variety melodrama. My victimhood seems petty. And the resentment I'd carried really *had* only hurt me and those around me. Her letter impacts me deeply.

Since returning home, I'd also received another piece of mail, one from Delta. A simple form letter, politely acknowledging my declination of the job. During the interview, they had told me that

I wouldn't know my airline hub city until six to nine months after being trained, let alone where in the United States I would need to move for the training itself. Because of all the recent big changes in my life, I knew that moving to an unknown city wouldn't create enough stability for me. My recovery was more important than this job. I had seen all the synchronicity surrounding my trip as a possible sign that I would get a new job, too. Even though my hopes for an adventurous travel job hadn't materialized, the trip had fulfilled unmet desires for friendship, connection, and continued amends.

From time to time, I take out my coin, rubbing it between my fingers and reading its tiny print once again. This brass coin—a token. The real treasure of my trip had come from forgiving and releasing myself from another part of my past. True recovery, I'm learning, requires more than just logging years without alcohol or drugs. I have to continue living up to the promises of my program. I need to keep on doing whatever it takes to deal with the underlying thought patterns that have perpetuated addiction.

I had been working for an oral and maxillofacial surgeon in the Belleville, Illinois, area since coming back from my trip to Georgia. One afternoon, I find myself in the plush, blue-gray office of another oral and maxillofacial surgeon—one I'd met 14 years ago at age 23.

Back then, I'd stopped shooting up, but hadn't yet entered

recovery. All the pain and insecurity that had created my addiction were firmly intact, and I'd been so desperate to do something that could make me feel better about myself. So when I'd learned of Dr. Rotskoff from my dentist, I jumped at the chance to correct my appearance.

When I met Dr. Rotskoff that first time, I'd played on his caring. I told him how I used to be a junkie. In my own mind, this was true, since I wasn't shooting up any longer, even though I was still using drugs and alcohol daily. At that time, telling him a story that I'd gotten "clean," and that I wanted to do something to take care of myself, he recommended an osteotomy to correct my underbite—a surgery where he would break my jaw, saw it in half, and move the jaw back—all at half the cost of what he usually charged. He'd even agreed to a long-term payment plan.

I woke up after the surgery in intensive care and didn't realize that my mouth would be wired shut. Everything was swollen from the inside out... my gums, my throat, even my lips. I couldn't talk and was completely freaked out.

My jaw remained wired shut for six solid weeks. I ate only a liquid diet, mainly alcohol, and still used drugs by crushing them up and sucking it in around the wires. I did this in spite of the fact that if I had vomited even once during that time, I would have choked to death. In my purse I carried wire cutters just in case.

But I hadn't cared about the risk. It mattered so much to me, this surgery. If I could've just gotten a little bit more attractive, maybe my life would finally get better.

Not surprisingly, though, I had neglected to pay the doctor in full for his already discounted services.

So I find myself sitting in his waiting room now, so many years later. At 37, I want to make amends. In my hand, I hold a check made out for the balance I still owe. I want to thank him for his kindness to me and apologize for the way I had taken advantage of him.

When he comes out, the look on his face tells me he doesn't remember me. As I reach to shake his hand, I give my full name. "Linda," he says with surprise. "I would never have recognized you!"

Recovery had changed me, down to the fact that my eyes had even turned from brown to blue-green since the time of my surgery with Dr. Rotskoff. Even more than this, however, I suspect he's picking up on a much bigger difference in me—the kind of change that comes from an internal transformation. The work I'm doing in recovery still often feels excruciating and requires everything I have to give, but it's finally paying off.

I explain to the doctor how I've been—truly—clean and sober for 11 years now, and I'm here to make amends for the way I had treated him. I also thank him for his patience with me and for being an important step in my journey to recovery.

He, like Frank from the pharmacy, indicates that the best repayment was that I was sober, clean, and doing so well. I left his office that day feeling lighter, free, grateful, and a little more like myself— the true me.

Some months later, something remarkable happens: Doctor Rotskoff offers me a job.

In a million years, I never would've predicted this turn of events. Not only do I have no inkling of an open position in his office, I also never could've dreamed that he would offer it to me, a former junkie who had preyed on his kindness. Once again, I'm witnessing the magic that comes from making a decision to turn my will and my life over to the care of God as I understood Him, one of the main commitments I re-state every time I go to a recovery meeting. Spirit's winding road, which had taken me to a job interview in Atlanta, Georgia, has now led me, without interviews or application, to another job.

Lesson & Blessing

#13

Redefining Success

As I've experienced so many times in my life, Spirit's flight plans had been perfectly on course, even if they didn't follow a direct route.

From the outside, my new life didn't match the standards of success. A marriage, a beautiful home, even my budding relationship with my mother after so many years of estrangement—everything I had used to prove to myself that I had made something of my life had vanished, almost overnight. In my rush to release Jeff, I had even left behind the friends I'd gathered in our life together, since I felt they were more his friends than mine.

I shock myself now to think of how artfully I dodged honesty during this time, especially with myself. And over the years, I judged myself harshly for this turn of events... *At my age, shouldn't my life have been a little further along? Had I been mad when I decided to drop everything in pursuit of this crazy notion that I could know myself better?*

Then I would talk myself down from this mind-ledge long enough to remember that I really did want to continue on the path I had chosen, even when I was stepping into the unknown and unable to see what was coming next. (Ha! Isn't it always unknown?) Fortunately, Spirit sent me little miracles of serendipity—the astrologer, the trip to Georgia, the unexpected job offer—to show me that I was cared for, protected, and held.

In addition, I was building inside myself a new definition of success. As I worked with my mind and heart, I came to see that my external achievements during my early phase of recovery had helped make me strong enough to reach for a whole new kind of success, one based on the internal journey rather than external markers. For that, the only road available would snake and twist through an inner landscape stocked with both trials and delights. No one could point to my internal victories and say, "You've really become successful." But *I* could.

Perhaps you've heard the famous quote attributed to Pierre Teilhard de Chardin: "We are not human beings having a spiritual experience. We are spiritual beings having a human experience." My version of this? "We are spiritual beings learning to embody here on Earth." The day-to-day experiences we have as humans help give shape and form to the Great Spiritual Energy we came from. Our task is so much greater and more noble than simply living up to the standards our culture has set for achievement. For me, success comes from staying true to this larger vision. It comes when I continue to actively learn and grow from whatever happens in my world. The act of watching this process unfold often offers the greatest blessings I know.

My trip to Georgia had not yielded a job. Yet it had been a raging success. I had mustered the courage to vanquish the dragon of resentment that lived in that old school castle in my mind, a conquest that I have carried forward every single day since and will carry for the rest of my life, as a greater sense of freedom.

Then I had serendipitously stumbled into the job with Dr. Rotskoff. Even if he had never offered me a job, my reunion with him was another success. Every time I made amends, I brought back into present time another piece of myself once stuck in the past.

If I aimed to know myself, then I had definitely found the right path.

It says in the "Big Book" that things will change, sometimes quickly, sometimes slowly, but they'll always materialize if you work for them. Though your emotions sometimes seemingly take over, this is an opportunity for you to slow down, breathe, and listen to what they're offering to you now.

How many times have you felt a momentary boost from an outer success, only to find the following day you're chasing the next one? This is what our overall society encourages, and we have a lot of practice living life this way.

However, the truest form of success that will last a lifetime is in building the inner home of peace that you can always return to. I encourage you to allow *everything* to be a part of the journey... the messiness is part of the unfolding into this peace, one moment at a time.

The Dormant Seed

*"The light of unconditional love awakens
the dormant seed potentials within us, helping them
ripen, blossom, and bear fruit, allowing us to bring forth
the unique gifts that are ours to offer in this life."*
~ John Welwood

As I stepped up to the podium, my hands are shaking. It's 1992, and a group of 300 women are gathered in Destin, Florida, for a conference: Women in Sobriety. Now all of them are looking at me expectantly, ready for what I have to say.

I take a deep breath, grabbing the podium to steady myself. This won't be easy. On the page in my hands I'm holding not just a speech, but a confession. I'm about to share some of my deepest, darkest secrets with a crowd of strangers.

"Never again do I want to see the face of a woman in pain, knowing that I'm the one who assisted in putting that pain there," I begin. I explain to the crowd how I had multiple affairs with other women's boyfriends and husbands.

Through bold words, my voice remains steady and clear. But shame burns my face as I speak. Will these women hate me by the time I finish this speech? Possibly. Still, I know that I have to share these important life experiences to benefit others. Another mantra of mine that I recite to myself during the talk: "In my vulnerability, my safety lies."

This topic has been on my mind a lot. Mom had gotten tangled in an affair that her religion had labeled a mortal sin. Her peers had judged her harshly, and the divorce that eventually followed years later logged another mortal sin on her record.

By this point, however, I hadn't cared about that notion. But what she had done had hurt me deeply. I had even hated her for it. Perhaps under the heavy judgments of those moral codes lie a salty grain of truth. If not actually a mortal sin that could send a person to hell, an affair was at least a choice that could hurt other people and create a sense of separation from oneself.

So why had I done it? If I knew the fallout so personally, why had I found myself stepping into the same trap? Hadn't I learned anything from Mom?

For years, I had prayed about this. I had asked, even begged, God to help me understand. I hadn't had a huge number of forbidden liaisons, but even one felt wrong to me. The topic consumed me as I searched to understand why I felt so compelled to make this choice. Over time, I had caught glimpses, flashes, of insight that helped me put the pieces together.

In my marriage to Jeff, I had yearned to go deeper with him. To experience honest, authentic communication about the things that didn't work between us. But I had no idea where to start. I kept thinking *he* needed to change. We could finally grow closer, I reasoned, if he would just open up to me.

I wasn't aware of my own part in this dance of secrecy. Only after I had left him did I begin to see my own tangled stories, a sticky web I had woven inside myself.

Like Jeff, I was keeping my own silence. I wanted to keep parts of my past under wraps. I carried a mass of unfelt emotions, stuff I hadn't yet dealt with. Instead of diving into that shark tank, though, I had reached for Jeff. Let him be my fix, the one responsible. If I dared vulnerability, if I really let him see all of me—the pain, the hurt, the ugly things I had done—surely he wouldn't love me anymore. I needed to live up to an old idea of "wife" I dragged around inside of me, one my mother had both taught me and then violated.

But my struggle to cover up the old wounds hadn't succeeded in getting rid of them. I felt the struggle and wounds with me all the time, shadowy figures following me through the streets. Sometimes my body ached to let them out. Perhaps this explained, at least in part, why I expressed this tension so physically, in sex.

Inside of an affair I could also talk freely. I didn't have to be a certain way since neither of us expected the connection to last. And the secrecy of an affair matched my own need for secrecy about my past. With a clandestine lover, I could create an illusion of truth, like a mirage that kept disappearing every time I arrived at it. In the pocket of space that an affair created, I touched the relief of honesty, but without ever really getting honest with myself.

So the silence of my childhood kept replicating itself in my life. Instead of dealing with the old hurt, I was acting it out. I had found another kind of drug. As with alcohol and hard drugs, my actions were hurting others and me. But just like those addictions, this pattern pointed to something much deeper in me that needed my full attention. Trying to be a "good wife" or a "good girl" wouldn't cut it. I had to get to the root of this.

Ongoingly during prayer and mediation, I'd begun asking God for help, and I would remember things from my past I'd buried. The sound of my father's voice, calling me a whore and a bitch. The unspoken rule that I needed to be thin and beautiful, with every hair in place, in order to catch a husband. The advertisements that had bombarded me all my life, loaded with messages about my body, my looks, my value as a woman. I could see threads of this suffering everywhere I looked.

The years of letting boys touch me began coming to mind, too. As a young girl, it had freed me for a few moments from the throbbing confusion of my life. I had been labeled "loose" by other kids. But the way those encounters made me finally feel alive in a dead world... that mattered more to me than anyone's judgments.

With age, the attention I got from men had turned from an

occasional thrill into a driving need. I lived for the flirting, the strokes to my ego and body from the opposite sex. They boosted my weak sense of self, just as they had in junior high.

Even in recovery, I had little interest in having children, though I loved being around them. While my reasons for this came from a variety of different experiences, not the least of which was the earlier forced abortion, I must also admit that the idea of pregnancy didn't appeal to me because I couldn't bear the idea of gaining weight. I had always used my beauty and the attention it brought me as evidence of my worth. I couldn't afford to lose it.

In time, my persistence in excavating this part of my personality down to its roots began to pay off. Near the end of my marriage, I decided to attend a 30-day, in-depth program focused on healing codependency, and I uncovered a surprising memory.

As a young child, I had gone many times with my family to visit my Great-Uncle Adam. He and his wife, Great-Aunt Ethel, lived in rural Pennsylvania, in a drowsy old Victorian two-story with a widow's peak and a large backyard.

The drive to Great-Uncle Adam's house always passed far too slowly. That morning, I had donned my Sunday best, clean white underwear, a ruffled dress, lace ankle socks, and perfect Mary Janes. But the care I had taken with my appearance had dissolved by now into restless anticipation. I fidgeted with the door buttons until my father hollered for me to stop, then fidgeted with the ruffles on my dress. I was bursting to be there. Great-Aunt Ethel would bake pies for us that she would cool in the windows. Great-Uncle Adam, a robust man with a kind face, would cuddle me, his special niece. From the kitchen window, I could watch him drive his riding lawn mower in tighter and tighter loops around their huge backyard. I would feel proud, since no one else I knew had a mower like this. I would also wonder anxiously when he would come inside again to play with me. No one could make me feel so important as Great-Uncle Adam did.

When we finally arrived, he and Great-Aunt Ethel would run to the front porch to greet us. I would turn into a cross between a movie star and an over excited dog every time. Even as an adult, I had thought of their place with fondness, a second fantasy home, where I had no responsibilities and I could do no wrong.

So I felt surprised during this healing program when a different version of my experience began to surface. I remembered descending a flight of old wooden stairs into their basement where Great-Uncle Adam shined his shoes. Cold concrete walls surrounded washing machines and a workbench, scattered with tools and unfinished projects. A single bulb cast interlocking rings of light and shadow around my great-uncle.

Great-Uncle Adam invited me to come sit on his lap. I happily complied.

I can't say what happened next. Inside me, I felt the tightening of a knot. Then I had a blank spot, like someone turned something off in my head. In a nanosecond, a collision of feelings burst through my mind in the musty air of that shadowy basement.

This feels wrong. But why?

After all, Great-Uncle Adam made me feel loved. And whatever this was, the thing he did to me, it felt good.

But it felt bad, too. Weird. Uncomfortable.

Which feeling can I trust? Does love always come with this kind of twist? Would I always have to pay for affection with a sacrifice?

Not long after this, my mother caught me masturbating and spanked me. Then, even more confusion and shame got linked to my sexuality.

These early sexual experiences had served as the wobbling framework around which I had built my identity, not just sexually speaking, but in every aspect of my womanhood. What would come after this could only turn out sideways... warped. Feeling simultaneously good in my body and guilty about it had gotten hard-wired.

When I began to deal with my own memories, I reflected on my mother's intense yearning to be loved by a man. It reminded me of the yearning I had experienced for attention from my Great-Uncle Adam. Had something like my encounter with him also happened to Mom? I had no way of knowing now. In fact, I suspect that even she wouldn't have known, or at least not have remembered it, if her experience was anything like my deeply buried memories.

I thought of my father's sudden emotional coldness to me after Mom's affair. Before then, I had been his princess. When he learned of the affair, though, he had begun treating me differently. I went from being "my angel" to "you bitch," practically overnight. I came to believe that he blamed me for not stopping Mom from having the affair. And all these years later, I still felt guilty, as though I, too, had somehow sinned.

When he had shut me out, I found myself desperate for his affection, just like Mom. Except that Mom had never known the love of her father at all. I felt compassion for us both as I reflected on all of this.

I also began tracing the pattern of infidelity through my father's lineage. His father had nursed a secret affair for two decades of his life. He had fathered two children with a woman who only a couple of Dad's siblings had known even existed until those children were mature men.

These secrets loomed over our family. I began realizing that as long as we keep them in the shadows, they would continue to crop up in our experiences, passing from one generation to the next as they had from my mother and my father to me.

But gradually I unraveled this. When I entered recovery, I had felt so much shame about being an addict. But being a woman had made it even more intense. At that time, society did not "allow" women to be addicts. Admitting to it meant that I had failed not only as a person, but as a woman. So even while I felt proud of myself for facing the beast of addiction, I also felt ashamed. I identified so strongly with the stereotypes I had attached to my name that I tried twice as hard as anyone I knew to live up to the models of womanhood I gleaned from my culture. I clung to Jeff and other men to prove to myself that I had not lost my feminine self.

As I continued recovery, I understood how much courage I had summoned to leave my marriage with Jeff. Only outside of it, could I begin to heal this wound of identity.

Talking about all this in front of a group of women helps me end the familial cycle of having affairs. Because of its healing effect on me as well as others, speaking at recovery gatherings becomes an important part of my life after my divorce. As I speak to these women in Florida, and many others, I share that: "Beyond any intellectual understanding, we all make mistakes. We react to our emotions." Forgiveness for myself dawns a little more each time I take the courageous leap into authentic vulnerability, a leap I had struggled with so much in my marriage, and hadn't even known was possible during addiction.

Eventually, though, I give up public speaking. For one thing, I begin to realize how tightly I'm clinging to my stereotype—my identity as a recovering addict. This had kept me safe in the early days of recovery when I had no inner resources and truly needed that new identity to replace an enslavement to substances. But as I heal, I realize that telling the story of my past, again and again, is keeping me locked in that way of seeing myself.

Some parts of me could never find full expression in that story alone. And I want to know all, not just part of me.

I also have another reason for letting go of the many speaking engagements that are filling up my calendar. At a certain point, I realize that I have come to rely on them to validate my worth just as I had relied for so long on men, alcohol, drugs, and more. In some ways, I'm still looking on the outside for what I need to learn to give to myself on the inside.

If I want a bigger life, I need a bigger self. Like a snake, I shed my skin once more to make the larger space my heart requires.

By this time, the healing taking place in me isn't arising simply from some abstract intellectual reflection on my earlier life, or even solely from the recovery meetings I'm still attending three or more times each week. Only by actively working with a wide range of tools do I begin to find some relief from the depression that has plagued me for so long. I take the physical aspect of recovery seriously.

I had been a smoker and soda drinker when I first entered my recovery program, but at less than 100 pounds, I gave those up when my sponsor had told me that I needed to gain weight and start eating healthy food. As the alcohol, drugs, and nicotine had left my system, a severe case of acne had spread out across my back. I realized that I needed to get to the bottom of this symptom, both because it looked so unattractive and because I sensed it was a signal that my body wasn't functioning properly.

This had put me on a quest. For many years, I had fueled myself on poison. How could I reverse what I had done to myself? While I still lived with Jeff, I had stumbled across a book on juicing written in the 30's by Norman Walker, a leader in juicing for health. Before long, I had purchased a used Champion Juicer® and filled our kitchen with carrots, celery, beets, and lemons. This was the 1980's in the Midwest.

People I knew looked at me like I had three heads when I talked about juicing and fasting, and Jeff had no interest in the practice either. But what other people thought of as madness, I knew to be guidance. So I pursued juicing and cleansing despite a lack of external validation, and learned to avoid talking about it with people who wouldn't understand.

Though the juicing helped, about five or six years into recovery, I still hadn't gotten rid of the acne. At the metaphysical bookstore I had begun to frequent, I learned about a chiropractor and acupuncturist, Dr. Patrick Fox, who focused on liver health. Dr. Fox put me on liver enzymes, and I began acupuncture treatment. I learned that my liver had taken the brunt of the impact of my addiction since it had to process all the toxins I had put in my body. Chinese medicine also taught me that the liver holds unexpressed anger, of which I had plenty. As I learned more, I added treatments like the Arise & Shine® Transformational Cleanse, and colonics, both which helped my liver recover.

Many of these physical treatments would stir up old emotions, which then sent me to therapy for greater understanding.

Many years into recovery, I found myself yet again telling a therapist that I felt crazy inside—the legacy of my childhood. When the therapist pressed me to explain what I mean, I couldn't.

"Crazy? Just crazy," I told her.

"Okay," she says, "I'm going to give you some words, and you tell me which one fits with what you feel like inside when you say you feel crazy."

This wise woman could see that I had never learned how to name my feelings. She said a few words, and then waited. One of the words is "confused."

Confused. Yes! Ever since my parents started taking me to psychiatrists, I had labeled that feeling of confusion inside me as crazy. Most of my life, I felt confused about the way I couldn't make my interior world match up with the world I found around me, and had numbed it to cope with this intense dissonance.

But confusion... that lives in a whole other dimension than crazy. I wasn't crazy. I was confused! This simple understanding brought me so much relief. The tight cords of judgment I had lassoed around myself began to loosen.

I shared with my therapist that a year before Jeff and I had separated, I had entered the 30-day treatment program for codependency where I uncovered the memory of my Great-Uncle Adam, as well as many of the insights about my sexuality and identity as a woman.

And during recovery, I did so many other things to get better. Network chiropractic. Massage. Sweat lodges in the Lakota tradition. Attending the Unity and Science of Mind churches. Reading Helen Schucman's "A Course In Miracles" and Louise Hay's "You Can Heal Your Life." When I became fascinated with crystals, Jeff and I went on a trip to Arkansas to dig for them. In time, I had moved out of survival mode. In the world of emotional and physical healing, I was exploring and actually finding answers to those deep, burning questions that had chased me all my life: *Who am I, and why am I here?*

Throughout these years, I had remained physically active, and I then began a love of running. After Mom died, however, I began to have trouble breathing. Running became harder and harder. When I learned that the lungs hold grief, I began to understand how my body was sagging under the emotional load of losing Mom. I realized that I needed something more than an inhaler to deal with this, which is what allopathic medicine would prescribe.

When my breathing problem continued to persist well into the fall of 1990, I began asking everyone I could think of what to do about it.

Someone recommends Rebirthing, a practice focused on breath work. I sign up for ten sessions with Jerrod Metz and I want more! In Rebirthing, I finally experience windows of time completely free from the depression that has been chasing me for so long. Rebirthing opens up a whole new world for me. I went there to be able to breathe better and release the grief, but it allows me to move emotional and physical energy that had been trapped inside me for my whole life. In one session, I expand momentarily into a sense that I'm connected with the entire world and feel utter peace. In time, these windows of contentment begin to last longer and longer.

Along with the practice, I also have a whole new community of people who care about the same things that I do. This helps immensely in my transition out of my marriage. Through the people I'm communing with in Rebirthing, I can see the parts of myself I had been searching for reflected back to me in a whole new way. My gifts and talents are more real to me as these friends notice them.

Through the Rebirthing community, I meet Evelyn. With short, copper hair and dancing blue eyes, the attractive Evelyn seems quiet and reserved at first, but as I get to know her, she opens up. Those sparkling eyes light up not only her own face, but the whole room around her for those who know her well. And she has a gentleness that instantly puts me at ease. The moment we meet, I feel drawn to her like the ocean tides to the moon.

From the start, she and I know an ease in our friendship that makes it natural for us to grow closer. She eventually becomes "Evie" to me. One day, I find myself sitting on the loveseat in the little room off Evie's kitchen with a steaming mug of tea in my hands. Evie sits in the armchair at my left, discussing what it would look like for me to become a housemate. She's inviting me to move into one of the spare rooms in her home!

Secretly, I feel surprised. No matter how many times people tell me they like me or want me, I never believe them—not fully. But now Evie, beautiful Evie, is asking me to move in with her. Inside, I'm thinking, "If Evie wants me, then I must be valuable after all."

Evie owns a brand-new, three-story house in an upscale suburban neighborhood of West St. Louis. With vaulted ceilings, clean white walls, and blond hardwood floors, the common areas of this home offer plenty of natural light and open space. Outside, we have a hot tub, and inside, a kitchen stocked with brand-new appliances where we gather for healthy meals or a cup of tea. Once again, I'm living in a beautiful home, something I'd thought couldn't happen for me as a single woman after I'd left Jeff. I feel the thrill of this small miracle almost every time I walk in the door for the first few months I live here.

Evie and I share the house in harmony with Pat, a woman in her late fifties who has no interest in Rebirthing or spirituality. But from time to time, Pat and I do something girly together like share makeup tips or put on facial masks. Her boyfriend and her active social life typically have her coming and going until late at night. We tease Pat, saying she should be setting a better example for Evie and me, since Evie is 10 years younger and I'm 20 years younger than her.

Age aside, I actually spend the most time at home. Once the wild party girl, I now revel in my solitude and time with Evie. Often we meet each other in the hallway, where we lean against the white open railing that overlooks the house's entryway. Here, we share stories..."You'll never believe who I saw last night..." which lead us into Evie's master bedroom. This huge space has fluffy carpet, a luxurious bathroom, and shelves lined with books. Jazz music plays in the background as we settle into her sitting area to talk. Our meaningful conversations in that little nook nourish me every bit as much as the juice I make in her kitchen.

My small room down the hall had been decorated with a child in mind. To sell the house, developers had covered it in animal print circus wallpaper. I wake up every morning to bright stripes, tumbling clowns, and exotic animals playfully peering through the bars of their cages. I'm returning to childhood and growing up all over again.

Outside the sanctuary of our bedrooms, a part of me still walks on eggshells in the rest of the house. Evie works as a nurse anesthetist with a strict sense of order and attention to detail that her profession requires. She likes everything just so, an echo of my military father. And I fear getting kicked out, not because Evie ever implies that I might, but because when faced with experiences that remind me of my childhood, I feel uneasy. To deal with my feelings, I pull inward, make myself small, and strain to do everything I can to please. And I continue to turn toward recovery and other healing modalities to learn to be with my emotions.

Luckily, I also have the whole finished basement of the house to myself. Evie had given that large space to me to use however I want. I make it my hangout, a place where I can spread out and unwind. Here, I can be myself.

A space like this fits my needs perfectly. In my marriage, I had learned a lot about myself, as well as how to be patient and work as a team. But I had never figured out my own passions in life. For this, I need more time alone.

Even if I had not fully understood it when we separated, I now know that this is why I had left my marriage. Discovering how to live from the inside out, instead of always outside in, is now the major task of my life. I had to take an active role in getting to know and experience my inner self. She's dying to burst from the plastic shell that had kept her rigid and breathless for so long. To do it, she needs time and space to emerge, and only I have the capacity to give those to her, no one else.

So I begin to explore deeper questions: *Is there really a God? What is that God like? What is bliss? What is prosperity, and how do I find it?* Without realizing it, I'm exploring my inner world.

Of course, this process doesn't always feel very fun. I still carry an ancient vulture on my shoulder that speaks in my father's voice. It says things like, "Who do you think you are, anyway?" And, "If you had any goddamn brains, you wouldn't know what to do with them." Or, "If you don't stop crying, I'm going to give you something to cry about!"

But other things begin to surface, too. Some as simple as my being able to say with confidence that I love Chinese and Thai food. It might not sound like a big step to others, but the feeling of revelation that it gives me comes from the fact that I've discovered that I can have an opinion about something, state it out loud, and even disagree with another person, and still be loved.

Teasing and joking begin to play a huge part in my relationships with the women in my house. Being around them makes room for my authentic feminine self to materialize, bit by bit. One day with them, one of them teases me and I hear myself laugh. The laugh goes all the way down into my belly and through me. I suddenly realize that for many years, every time I laughed I'd been thinking: *Who's laughing? Is it really me, or am I just faking it?* Now I know, however, that my real laughter fills me... my own, real laugh. I also learn how to laugh at myself. I've stopped taking myself so seriously.

At work, something is happening, too. Even though I had never earned more than a G.E.D., I keep getting better jobs with greater responsibilities and better compensation. A physical therapist who comes on a regular basis to the surgeon's office where I'm working had gotten to know me and encourages me to apply for a job in the practice that he owns with three other men. Soon, I find myself in a new position in that upscale office, in large part because of his recommendation. I buy new nice clothes and the car I want. I travel. I get even more satisfaction, though, from knowing that my contribution matters. No one ever asks me about my education; they see me for my business sense, warmth, and kindness, and the skills that I have to offer.

Since running had become less interesting, I decide to take up inline skating that then takes me to inline racing. The sport gets me out nearly every day into St. Louis' Forest Park, close to my work on South Brentwood Boulevard. Huge, old trees yawn over the five-kilometer trail, where I can smell lilacs in spring and watch the leaves change color in autumn. In nature, I recharge and reflect on the beauty of my life.

On top of all this, the many years of fasting, cleansing diets, colonics, and juicing are finally beginning to catch up with me, the way the drugs once had, but in reverse. I'm healthier, stronger, and living with more functional organs. My body is repairing the damage I had done.

One morning in late winter 1992, I wake up after completing an Arise & Shine® Transformational Cleanse, and the whole world has changed. I feel light and expanded... my lifelong depression has lifted. I can't quite put this into words because I had lived with shame, fear, loneliness, inadequacy, and confusion for so long that it had simply felt like a part of me—like a strange extra limb I had resigned myself to accept. That morning, though, I feel a change in me like a pressure lifting, as when a heavy front clears. I can breathe. I can think. My internal weather forecast reads "blue skies."

However, my many years of struggle have taught me to see easeful days like this one the way many people see the rough ones. *Eventually this too, will pass.*

But it doesn't pass. A week goes by, and I'm actually feeling optimistic. I notice that I care more about other people and less about rehashing what a bad person I am. The sensation still seems strange, though. I don't yet trust it, and I don't share it with anyone else.

One night, I go out with friends, including a man I had met in recovery when he was just 18 years old. He had come to the house as a casual friend when I had been married to Jeff, and I had bumped into him at social gatherings for years. After an evening of dancing, he and I go out to a local breakfast joint to keep the fun alive. In the wee hours of the morning, I find myself eating an omelet across the table from this handsome man. He's older now, of course, but still much younger than anyone I had ever considered dating. What exactly am I looking for in a man, anyway, he wants to know? I think he might see me as more than a friend.

"What do you think?" he asks me in the car on the drive home. "Am I old enough yet for you to go out with me?" Passing street lights flash across his ginger hair as we drive, creating an on-and-off strobe. I remember his muscular arms around me when we were dancing earlier in the evening, his sturdy, stocky frame sweeping me over the floor. And I already know, he has a really cute tushy. But he's 15 years my junior, and I find myself once again in a tug of war between cultural messages telling me this is wrong, and what my heart is feeling.

With much trepidation spiraling inside with the confusion of this tug of war, I finally say, "Sure, let's explore this."

It's December 23, my mother's birthday, and he kisses me. I have a thought that Mom has something to do with this from the other side.

Whether or not she does, John and I have a great time together. He has sisters my age, so he knows my music and loves it, and feels comfortable around the culture I was raised in. His parents adore me and see me as an asset in his life. This 25-year-old young man pulses with life. At his age, I had been drugged out of my mind. Now, I discover how it feels to be 25 and sober.

I notice, too, the way he cares for me. He opens doors and anticipates what I might need. Other men had loved me before him, but I had never been able to let myself feel it. Something warm grows inside me, soft and glowing, filling up the spot where I had once put alcohol's stinging heat.

Eventually, I begin to admit to myself that the good days are starting to pile up, just like so many miserable ones had in my past. I wake up on my fortieth birthday and realize I feel joy.

In my ongoing recovery program, we read a series of statements at the end of each meeting that comprise the promised rewards of working the program. As part of that recitation, I repeat, more times than I can possibly count, the statement, "We will not regret the past nor wish to shut the door on it." Every time I say it, I hope all over again that it may one day become true for me. But deep inside, I don't think I ever actually believed that day would come.

After 15 years of recovery, now it has.

Lesson & Blessing

#14

Your Healing Belongs to Everyone

I now know that my healing isn't just *my* healing. I had lived under a filter—gray and ashy—the veil of depression, despair, and addiction that had permeated my family at least as far back as my grandparents, and probably further. Until I pierced that veil, all I could do was relive their worn out stories, trapping time in an endless coil around me.

During this period of my life, I began to heal on a whole new level. I learned what's now called Emotional Intelligence, becoming aware of what I was *really* feeling. For example, I was able to articulate that the emotion of "shame" was the feeling that had weighed on me for so many years. I learned how to be with myself and appreciate the value of alone time. And I learned how to enjoy positive, joyful relating.

And as I healed, I was healing for all of us.

I was healing for all the women before me—my mother, my grandmothers—who felt confused about how to receive and give love.

I was healing for all the men before me—my father and grandfathers—who had turned to alcohol to drown out their feelings. They had used it to silence the despair they felt about how to handle what life had thrown at them.

I was healing for my brother. Earlier on, I had left a Big Book at his house and had no idea that I would ever hear from him about it. One afternoon later that summer, I had been sunbathing on a lawn chair outside my country home when he called me..."I need help," I heard his voice say, in a quivering tone I rarely heard from him. He wanted to get free from alcohol addiction. Years later, he confessed, "Linda, I knew if you could get sober, then anyone could. That's what gave me the courage to call you." And he, too, remains sober to this day.

I was even healing for Great-Uncle Adam. What was Great-Uncle Adam harmed by that made him susceptible to this type of action? First, I felt my own hurt and wounding, and then I could open up and recognize that there was a lot more going on than only *my* hurt and wounding. When I opened up the curiosity in me and began to heal the secrets of the past, I became more whole. I began asking *What else is possible?* without the story that Great-Uncle Adam is *only* a perpetrator, for example. I see him, instead, as someone who was himself hurting and probably had his own wounding in childhood that he was unconsciously repeating.

I had been so confused about my feminine identity throughout my life. My primary influences included my father's messages about women—that they need to be thin and subservient. And, my behavior toward men was modeled to me by my mother, who's mother died at 49, long before her feminine identity was fully formed, let alone that of my mother's. If we're repeating our family patterns, where does it begin?

We don't know how far back the messages go. But I know now that the patterns and messages end with me. My mother's parents divorced in 1939 when she was only 9 and an only child. Her longing to be loved was apparent to me in the way she behaved. My grandmother was a single mother in a time when that wasn't accepted. She had crippling arthritis and could barely take care of herself, leaving my mother starved for love and chronically looking outside of herself for a sense of wholeness.

This inheritance on my mother's side, mixed with the messages from my father, left me bereft of a sense of my own inner brilliance, without the constant reflection from the outside-in.

The biggest transformation of my life would come through my recovery journey as my inner light began to take up the most space, and my incessant seeking for outside-in acceptance and love dropped away.

Along the way, I wondered about my family of origin—the people who had lived and died before me—my ancestors, the ones who had paved the path upon which I had walked and suffered. As my recovery continued, instead of only paying attention to their suffering, I began to imagine them with me, cheering me on from the other side. What were they saying? One day, instead of thinking that I was only imagining the soft, light whispers from other realms, I decided to let them speak. Like a flock of birds choking the sky, they squawked with a flood of messages, downloading into me.

"You carry a seed," the voices said. "It has stayed dormant in you—until now."

This seed carried the hopes and dreams of my family, the greatest longings of all my ancestors. Until then, I hadn't realized that not only individuals, but our family had a soul, too. One that had been guiding me. Without knowing it, I had entered on a journey to know and fulfill not just my own desires, but the longings of our shared soul as well.

I watered our seed, not knowing when, or even if, it would begin to sprout. Instead of pushing it down, I began allowing my soul's essence to speak together with theirs.

And the seed did sprout. With its tender green leaves, that seed began breathing new life into the old, tired stories I had inherited. I continued to see my family respond to my healing, making steps of their own in response to mine. By watching them, my own healing accelerated all over again. Back and forth we went, creating a new positive feedback loop.

Wholeness was sprouting in me, in us. Even my ancestors, the ones whose names I never knew, spoke to me of healing. With wordless voices, they called to me. They held me. Instead of getting stuck in a negative loop as we had in my early years, we were rising upward together, our shared soul fulfilled.

And when I sat down to begin writing this book, I

realized that I was also healing for you. And healing has a ripple effect. This possibility propelled me to share my deeper truths, the raw pain of my experiences, and the alchemy of discovering the blessings that were already embedded in life's lessons every step of the way.

You, too, are healing for yourself, and for everyone. And as I often like to say: "When you heal yourself, you heal the community." This occurs naturally, almost by default. In Latin, community means "the place where we are received." As your journey continues, notice the new ways you're received by others as your inner brilliance gets the space it needs to sprout and grow.

Conversations With My Father

"And the day came when the risk to remain tight in a bud was more painful than the risk it took to blossom."
~ Elizabeth Appell

By now, I regularly find myself at the ironing board, a habit woven into the strands of my DNA by my military father. By age five, I could bounce a quarter off a bed I had made, just the way my father had trained me. Now in my forties, I still won't wear a shirt to work without perfect creases.

But inside, I keep finding wrinkles of confusion that I can't seem to iron out. Things in my life are so much better. But I still haven't completed making things right with my father.

"Dad," I hear myself say, my voice shaky as I balance the phone receiver between my shoulder and ear. The hot iron in my opposite hand glides in wide strokes over the back of a white shirt and I continue. "We need to talk."

Silence.

"I need to tell you the stories I tell myself. What I tell myself you thought about me and what I believe you think happened between us."

For many years, I'd been slowly training my father to know what I would and wouldn't accept from him. At age 31, six years into my recovery, I had come to his home wearing a loose linen outfit I had bought in Montreal that made me feel beautiful and stylish. Without thinking, he had rattled off, "That dress looks like a goddamned gunny sack on you."

Instantly, heat rose in my chest. I turned slowly, looking straight at him. "You will never speak to me like that again," I told him through a stare. "If you don't have anything nice to say to me, then don't speak to me at all. I don't want your opinion again." With this, I had left his house. Taking that step had been important for me at the time. Finally, I was respecting myself. I refused to let my father terrorize me any further.

But somewhere along the way, I had come to realize how empty and automatic my father's insults had been. Just as I had listened to myself tell Jeff to wash his hands, repeating my mother's words without even thinking about them, my father had likely been rattling off insults from his own childhood and military training. Yet, I began to see these repetitive statements not as the cruel words of a father who believed me an idiot; rather they had come straight out of the military playbook. He had heard this kind of stuff daily since he entered the service at sixteen. In fact, his own father, a coal miner who had raised his son on toughness, alcohol, and rancor, had likely used these epithets on my father long before the military entered the picture. By the time I came along, words like these had become so mechanical to my father that I doubt he even heard himself say them anymore.

This insight softened my heart to him. After all, I knew firsthand the challenge of breaking inherited family patterns. I had worked hard to find my way out of them, but my father came from an era that hadn't offered him the personal development option.

Most of my life, I'd fumed at him for the ways he had spoken to me as a child. But at age 40, I've now practiced over and over making choices that have helped create the "better life" that the *Presence* had promised. I have proven to myself I can set boundaries that I don't let him cross. If I still suffer from the insults he had thrown on me in childhood, it happens now because I'm repeating the echo of his slurs inside my own head. I'm now the only terrorist in my life. And therefore, I'm now the only one who can end the terrorism.

I begin seeing that I've been responding primarily to the emotions behind his words, but had never really asked him if he really means what he says. Underneath his reflexive volley of toxic words, what does *he* really think and feel?

In my thirties, he and I had taken a long drive together to a family wedding. To get through it, I decided to act like a reporter. I would be at a neutral party and interview him about his life. And I had been surprised at his openness with me. On this road trip, he became real to me for the first time, not just my father, but a person. He had once been a teenager, with all the struggles of that era and time in one's life, which I had of course faced in a different form. Before that, he had been a kid. Like I had realized with my mother, my father's parents, culture, and experiences had shaped him, too. It was time for me to clear out the old ideas so that we could have a new relationship.

The memory of this drive ten years prior gives me courage. He had shared himself so honestly with me then. Surely, we can find a way to speak to one another again this way. The only way I can imagine changing my story about him will come from understanding him better. This will be for my own sake, as much or even more than for his.

So I call him that day while standing at the ironing board. Our conversation is short, but my father agrees to talk more in person. We arrange a time over the weekend when we can meet face to face.

The following Saturday afternoon, I find myself standing on his front porch, shuffling my feet back and forth nervously as I wait for him to open the door. When he answers, the dark insides of his little house cast a blanket of shadow over him, so that I can hear, but not see, him speak. From the tone of his voice, though, I know my commanding father feels as shy as I do today. A single hand, marked with the brown spots of age but as robust as it has ever been, pushes through the shadows, into the afternoon light as he opens the screen door across its threshold.

Can I do this? Do I really have the courage to keep my focus on the possibilities between us, instead of on what had been damaged or lost? I take a deep breath and step through the open door.

"Do you want something to drink?" he asks me as I stand in his small front room. Here sits my father's overstuffed recliner. All my life, my father's recliner had held pride of place. I had even once known my frugal father to give away an almost-new recliner when he had decided it didn't feel right. No one in our family would dare sit in his chair.

In retirement, that chair had become even more important. Like the sun at the center of planets, his life now orbits around this spot. Routinely, his second wife carried cold drinks from the kitchen to this chair, where he passed most of the weekends watching football games, other sports, or old movies on the TV set across the room. On weekdays, he watched everything from talk shows to the news—whatever he found that could keep his attention.

As he settles into his chair now, he reaches for the remote to switch off the TV I take my own seat on the edge of the couch next to him. Age had treated my father kindly. Even at 65, he's still starting each day with a vigorous bike ride that keeps him sturdy and fit. The strong presence he carries to match his strong physical constitution now fills up the space between us.

Since that call to him while ironing earlier in the week, I had been mulling over what I would say. Sitting next to him now, though, muddles all my planned speeches. As a kid, I had never hesitated to tell him how much I hated him. "I wish you would die!" I had screamed on more than one occasion. I had wanted him to hurt as deeply as I did. But now, I ache to show him compassion. I know that no one had ever given him a chance before now to see things in a different light.

I choose my words gingerly, feeling into each one the way I might test an icy pond before giving it my full weight.

"You know I believe I chose you as my father coming into this life."

"Yes..." he sheepishly responds, already unsure of where we're going.

"You know how I believe we each have 100% responsibility for our choices, right?"

A small nod.

"Well, Dad, I have all these stories I tell myself about how you spoke to me, how you treated me physically, what happened with Mom."

He nods again. I feel unsteady, but I have to do this.

"I blamed myself a lot for Mother's affair," I finally exhale into the room. The sentence pulls on my insides like barbed wire. "I was living with her when you went to Thailand. I thought I should have stopped it from happening, but I didn't."

I pause, waiting for the surge of almost-shed tears to pull back inside me.

"When you came home, I thought you blamed me, too. You had never beaten me before. Is that true, Dad? Did you blame me?" Now, I really am crying.

And my father begins to explain. "I don't blame you for this," he says. "In my mind, none of it was ever your fault."

"I'm really sorry," he continues. Regret and sadness cross his face like a cloud passing over the sun. Looking at that face, I no longer have any questions in my mind. He had never meant to harm me.

"I just didn't know," he goes on. "I didn't know how to be with a little girl."

I remembered the way he spent all his time with men, leaving his Air Force job for evenings in the bars with his cronies, where they drank and told war stories into the dark of the night. Whatever he knew about women, how to be around them, what to say or how to act, had come to him through the tightly scripted social mores of his time.

We talk more that day. But at a certain point, my questions begin to dissolve before I can speak them. Love melts me. I can feel it in the room. I see it on his face. Something is happening—between us, to us, around us. We have found new ground.

This conversation would become the first of many in the years ahead. The urge to ask him questions would hit me all over again, usually when I was ironing. Then I would call, and we would arrange a time when I could come.

By our third conversation, my father apologizes to me for raising me like a military man instead of a girl. As we talk through our past, I start to understand his love for me. For one thing, he had never given up on me through those years of addiction, paying for my time in psych wards, giving me money that had bailed me out of bad drug deals, in spite of the fact that I had lied to him about why I needed it, even helping me pay for the jaw surgery I had wanted so badly. Just after Mom died, Ron had called Dad and his wife, knowing how much I was struggling, and they all came to the celebration for my 10th anniversary of recovery.

Now 1994, 15 years into recovery, I finally share with him that I know what a challenge I must have posed for him. This by-the-book military man had ended up with a wild, drug-addicted alcoholic for a daughter. Yet never once has he turned his back on me. Surely his love, even if it hadn't looked the way I had wanted, had been an important force in my survival.

Even so, I can't say he suddenly becomes the father I had always dreamed of, at least not overnight. He still commands. He demands. And he doesn't hesitate to give me his lectures on exactly how I should live my life.

"You haven't invested enough money for your future," he declares. But his force of will doesn't topple me anymore.

"Dad, I'm going to tell you how I've invested my money," I answer. "I've invested it in my health, psychotherapists, education, personal development training, furthering my career, and supporting my recovery. I know you can't yet understand this, but I've made the greatest investment anyone can ever make. I've spent it on healing work so that I would still be alive today. It's why I can talk to you the way I do, why we can have a relationship now. The way I see it, I made an investment that we can't put a dollar sign on even if we tried."

Finally, the pieces of my life have made a pattern that makes sense to me. At age 17, I had written in my journal, "I will not settle for less than what I'm worth." It had taken me all this time, and every resource I had, to understand what those words meant. I made it to this place because I didn't skip over any of the healing resources I had invested in along the way. It's a bit like connecting the dots in a coloring book. You don't know what the outcome of the picture will be until you reach the last number.

I've been dating a man named Steve, someone I had met through Rebirthing, for about four years now. From the beginning, however, our relationship had felt less like love and more like tug-of-war. If I move close, Steve moves away. If I move away, he moves close.

By this point in my healing journey, I begin to realize that my relationship with Steve is a lot like with my relationship with my father. Like him, Steve has two children and works hard to provide for them. Also like my father, Steve keeps up a stoic front. He sends me mixed messages—one day warm, the next day cold and distant. I begin to feel that love with Steve hovers just beyond my grasp. Even when I feel Steve's affection, I brace myself for the moment when he'll undoubtedly yank it away again.

I came to see that I had felt exactly the same way toward my father after he came back from the war. Many times, I respond to Steve just as I had to my father. I cry, beg, or plead. One minute, I might say something hurtful to him to get his attention, and the next, cry and tell him how sorry I feel. Why can't he just give me his love without so many conditions?

One Sunday afternoon, as I drive away from a particularly difficult encounter with Steve, I find myself asking God, "Why the heck am I doing this? Why am I stuck in such a difficult relationship?"

In response, I hear a wise voice inside me say, *You can't leave this relationship until you discover the deeper reason for why it hurts.*

This answer seems similar to the reason I'm still in St. Louis, even though I have such different values and interests than many of the people I know here. Spirit shows me that I can't leave the area until I've fully healed the past with my father. And it seems that my relationship with Steve is showing me the way.

It would take years for me to unpeel the layers of old pain that my relationship with Steve brought to the surface. Countless rounds of breaking up and getting back together with him kept me on a rollercoaster of emotional highs and lows. After one particularly tumultuous breakup, he calls to tell me he'll be having surgery soon. "Would you come support me?"

My heart goes out to him, so I say yes.

But when I find myself with Steve again, I see clearly: Nothing has changed. Nothing will ever change between us. I've had enough. All those talks with my father to heal our relationship have gradually healed my relationships with all the men throughout my life. Finally, I've truly learned that I no longer need to replay the dynamics with my father with other men.

After his surgery, Steve and I choose to part paths.

Lesson & Blessing

#15

Connection Heals Addiction

My conversations with my father transformed our relationship. As I became clearer, so did he. My openness fueled his, which then opened me up even more. Eventually, I would tease him, saying that I owe a thank-you letter to Oprah who had given him back to me. After he retired, he had started watching her show. It became not only his entertainment, but his education—a place where he could see that others cared about healing just as I did. From the show, he learned new ways of seeing his own life.

In his own quiet way, he was building a bridge back to me just as I had been building one to him. Eventually, we met in the middle.

These conversations did so much more than change our relationship, however. I had created relationships like the one with Steve in an unconscious effort to complete what had happened in childhood. But talking with my father took me straight to the root of this pain. I could more directly access my long-time yearning for his love and approval, which I thought I had lost so young when my mother had her affair. As we spoke to each other, I realized I had never truly lost his love. Our conversations changed this story. And with it, the destructive cycle in my relationships also changed.

I received healing beyond this, too. As my father and I related to one another differently, I related to myself differently. I already knew myself as a daughter beloved of her mother. Now, I had also reclaimed my identity as Daddy's precious girl. The volume of his harsh insults in my head began to turn down. The words melted into a space of quiet calm. I had more confidence than ever.

In all honesty, talking to my father about our past didn't come easily. Nobody wakes up on a beautiful day and says, "Wow, it's gorgeous outside. I think I'll look at my childhood trauma." For most of us, we face the demons only when we've finally gotten fed up with the discomfort they cause.

You can invoke this power to heal in your life. It starts with recognizing, not just intellectually, but with your whole being—body, mind, and spirit—that your perceived problems never truly come from outside of you. They never did, and they never will. *You* are ground zero. Within you, lies the power to change the way your life plays out—within you and nowhere else.

Also, as we explore having difficult conversations with others in your life, remember that lasting healing doesn't come from talking alone. That is, not through rational talking or thinking. You have to access the emotional part of the body, where the wound happened, and feel it. Then, when we can feel that others feel our authenticity, a deeper healing can take place. When we came together, my father and I both entered this territory through the gateway of vulnerability and possibility. I arrived with curiosity, without a need to shame him. I came with openness and without judgment. And what resulted is that we shared a space of heart connection. In this place, logic and reason held little power.

To enter a place like this with someone with whom you have a painful story takes courage and skill, as well as a fair degree of personal healing. The first conversation to have isn't with the others in your life whom you have impacted or whom have impacted you. Rather, begin with your own inner healing first, as the recovery steps indicate.

When I approached my father 15 years into my recovery, I consciously chose not to blame him for anything that happened between us. Instead, I spoke only about my own perspectives on the past and my own perceptions of our shared experiences. If I had come to these conversations with anger, I never could have resolved this old pain. I would simply have reiterated it. When we go to someone with anger, they're likely to shut down, go into old patterns, protect themselves, and perhaps retaliate.

But I could only do this after years of developing my capacity to witness myself—my thoughts, emotions, and behaviors—through the practices of recovery and the many holistic modalities. In addition to countless hours on the meditation cushion, I had also logged many hours receiving professional support. This helped me see more clearly the many stories I'd been telling myself, such that I could eventually see through them and stop needing to repeat them. Rebirthing and talk therapy supported me tremendously with this, but I believe that *all* the modalities I engaged with—from bodywork to juicing, astrology, sweat lodges, Pranic Healing, and more—brought me to the place where I could reconcile with my father and finally learn to live in the present moment.

Even so, the essential ingredient in my healing came from the same place I've pointed to many times throughout this book: *learning to see myself, life, and others in a new way.* And this became more and more possible not only through the many therapies and cleanses, but through the continual presence of grace working in seen and unseen ways.

The more I chose to see my father and our past differently, the more we both healed. To do this, I had to reach for compassion. Why had my father behaved so harshly with me? What did I most want from him, and how could I give it to myself and him first, instead of insisting he give it to me? I realized that I was given the gift of recovery; and recovery allowed me to realize that so much was possible if I was willing to embody the learning. The program offered me the prayer of St. Francis of Assisi, that it's better to understand than to be understood, to console than to be consoled. And I took that to heart.

At any moment, no matter where you're at in your own healing journey, you can ask yourself open questions about someone who has harmed you. If you find them difficult to even consider, you're not alone. I also found them hard to swallow. I had to allow time for the healing between Dad and me to unfold. As I became able to receive him as another human being doing the best he could, I began to understand that, just like me, he didn't have the road map to life.

I encourage you to keep reaching. Not because it's "the right thing to do." Not because you believe you *should.* I encourage you to stretch for this place of compassion simply because of how well it will pay off for you and those around you. In the reaching, I also encourage you to continue surrendering to the great unknown—what I've shared in these pages as grace or Spirit—which is continually reaching for you.

Reconciling with my father has brought freedom, a kind of freedom that I hadn't even envisioned was possible before I experienced it. Anyone can have this kind of freedom, or more. Anyone who's willing to say yes to recovery and walk the journey of its unfoldment.

Taking Flight

*"Love brings up everything unlike itself,
so the soul can purge itself of our barriers to love."*
~Marianne Williamson

"**M**ark's gone."

I pause. The voice on the phone belongs to my friend Rebecca who's also close to my dear friend Mark. Why is she calling me at work?

"What do you mean he's gone?" I ask. "I know he's out of town," I explain. He and I had talked multiple times about the business trip he was on, but the tone in her voice puts me on edge. Has something happened?

"No, Linda, he's gone," she repeats. "He's dead."

Dead? He can't be dead. I had just attended a birthday party with him on Saturday night. Before we left the party, Mark handed me the key to his apartment, encouraging me to come over there for alone time if I needed it while he went away. Then I talked to him again on Sunday, just hours before his Monday departure.

I sit mute. My mind invents a horrible plane crash, a car accident, a holdup at gunpoint. What tragic event could have taken one of my best friend's lives so suddenly?

But the answer to that question is worse than I could have imagined.

When Mark didn't show up for work at the remote job site, coworkers had started calling his house, where they got no answer. Someone from work came to his apartment to make sure nothing had happened to him. When they heard a noise inside the apartment and no one came to the door, Mark's coworker called the police.

Eventually, the police broke into his home, but not in time. Shortly before, and less than two days after we had last spoken, Mark hung himself. When police released his body from the rope, it was still warm.

Clearly, Mark had not committed this act on impulse. He had installed an anchor in the doorframe where he hung himself, one strong enough to support his weight. He had even laid down plastic underneath. Attention to details like these showed he had likely been planning his suicide for a while.

As the news of it sinks in, the world around me collapses. How could I have missed this? Mark is one of my best friends. We had just been laughing together. He never gave me the smallest clue that he even felt sad, never mind feeling suicidally depressed. How long had he suffered in silence? Had I just been so wrapped up in myself that I didn't pay enough attention? Didn't he know he could tell me anything? That I wouldn't judge him?

In the months after his death, I scour through my memories for some clue that this had been coming. The only thing I can find out of place had been a visit from him at my work just a handful of days before he died. Close to lunchtime, our receptionist told me that I had a visitor. I remembered looking through the glass at the front desk to see him waiting for me. He looked gray... ashy. A weird feeling came over me, one I couldn't explain. The feeling left as quickly as it came.

He wanted to take me to lunch, he explained. Mark had never shown up at my work before... had never taken me out to lunch during the week like this. It struck me as odd, out of place.

But I had overlooked it. Our lunch had seemed normal enough, so I brushed off my premonition.

Had I failed him? If I had, there's nothing I can do to change it.

Dammit. I know all about feeling suicidal. I understand the tangle of pain that would drive someone to do something this drastic. If anyone can relate to his suffering, I can. Yet I never had the chance to say any of this to him.

I struggle to understand. We had such a close friendship. How could I have missed the signs?

I feel like an imploding star, folding in on myself in despair and self-blame. In the place Mark had once occupied in my heart, I now find a huge gaping hole. All the light and joy of the last few years disappears into the gravity field of his unexpected death.

Mark and I had made such good memories together. We loved going dancing, our bodies abandoned to the throbbing beats of electronica in a local club. Pulsing lights captured the motion of his slender frame in halting progression, like time-lapse photography. And the memories of coming over to his Forest Park apartment, an old red brick mansion converted into smaller units, stay near.

One afternoon, I had stopped by when Mark was baking. As I knocked on his door, the smell of rising bread permeated the hallway. But the scene inside could have made Martha Stewart's lip curl. Somehow, Mark had mis-timed the rising process and his bread had exploded with such force that bits of it had even stuck to the 20-foot ceiling. This evidence of his misadventures would stay up there for a long time, since cleaning dried, sticky bread dough at such a height posed a nearly impossible task. We laughed so hard that we both nearly cried. If he had harbored any hopes of becoming a baker, I suggested he abandon them.

But now that Mark is gone, remembering these happy times hurts. I reach for the phone wanting to tell him something funny that had just happened, and catch myself. With one of my best friends now gone I no longer have this close confidant... a person who keeps my secrets and gives me reliable advice.

And he had played another role for me. I had always looked up to Mark—followed his lead. He taught me about holistic healing and health, about environmental stewardship. Earlier that year, he had given me a cloth grocery bag. Despite weird looks and annoyed sighs from store clerks in 1996 conservative St. Louis, he insisted on reusable bags for every purchase.

Simply seeing that bag hanging in my home hurts and I burst into tears. I wonder, how can I be so devoted to holding onto an old cloth bag, yet have failed to hold onto such a dear friend? Losing Mark hits me hard.

Even in the thick of this crisis, however, Spirit is watching out for me.

Just a few months before he passed, Mark and I had gone over to the home of some dear friends, Julie and Craig. They had just had a baby and they wanted me to be able to get to know their child. They wanted to know if I could move in with them and serve as a live-in fairy godmother, sharing in both the work and the joys of caring for a newborn.

When we came to look at the space they were offering, Julie and Craig showed me to a huge, unfinished attic with dormers and plenty of room. Generously, Craig offered to finish it to my liking. I knew instantly that I wanted to share my life with this family for as long as it made sense. I couldn't explain why—it just felt so right.

It comes at just the right moment. On an early spring day, I haul my boxes up the stairs into the attic of Julie and Craig's house. I feel in the moment that Spirit has provided for me in the form of this loving support—before I even had any inkling of how much I would need it.

What a miracle! This miracle of a loving home had materialized out of thin air. Now that Mark is gone, these supportive friends give me not only the gift of a home, but the support when I most need it. The pain that this period of my life brings up is almost too over-whelming at times.

I find it hard to go to meetings and begin spending more and more time alone. Yet despite this being one of the most tragic experiences in my entire 17 years of sobriety, I still choose to simply feel my feelings. Nothing, not even the depth of this despair, can send me back to drugs or alcohol.

Craig works as a chef, so for the first time in my recovery I don't need to cook every meal for myself. I list the groceries that I want on a white board in the kitchen and add my money to the kitty. Then delicious food "magically" appears on the table at mealtimes. I also get to spend lots of time with their baby, Andrew, a beautiful being. Through my reading of mystical texts and teachers, I know that he had just come from that realm of light and perfection—the same one that I had experienced when I left my own body after attempting suicide. The magic and preciousness in this family experience soothe the hurt of losing Mark so unexpectedly.

"Babaji told me to do a Mundan Ceremony," I tell Nancy as I emerge from the altered state of a Rebirthing session. While in that ethereal place, I had seen a vision of the East Indian saint, Haidakhan Babaji, whom I considered an important teacher and guide. In my mind's eye, Babaji was laughing and doing backflips and telling me to do a Mundan Ceremony, the Indian spiritual practice of shaving the head to mark a milestone or auspicious day in one's life. In Babaji's tradition, the hair holds the "egoic mind"—the I-don't-need-you-God attitude—that many of us are coming up against on the spiritual path. Shaving off all the hair communicates to Spirit a total surrender, an attitude where literally nothing stands between our smaller self and the Highest Self, which is always beaming down light on the crown of the head.

"So Babaji wants you to shave your head, eh?" Nancy replies. She had been my first trainer in Rebirthing since I had discovered the practice seven years before, and she's just returned to town for a workshop and to offer individual sessions. When I hear she's coming, I know I need to see her. I had continued to experience great difficulty understanding Mark's choice, and the confusion and self-incrimination I was feeling not having been able to be there for him. I know that I need support to both accept his decision to end his life, and understand that it had nothing to do with me.

The timing of Nancy's visit also strikes me as significant. I know that in many spiritual traditions, the number seven signifies the place where Heaven and Earth come together, signifying a chance to understand the hidden, underlying truth. I had begun Rebirthing at the end of my marriage seven years prior, when grief over both the loss of my marriage and my Mom's death had ruled my life. Now I face another loss that sends me to my knees all over again. I sense a cycle in my life is coming full circle.

"Yeah," I tell Nancy, "Babaji told me to shave off all my hair. But I'm not doing that. It's crazy."

I had just received a promotion at my job at a sports medicine physical therapy corporation where I have a visible role in serving well-known athletes and other local notables. I know I can't show up there with a bald head. That was that.

The next day, I gather with many familiar faces from the Rebirthing community for a group Rebirth workshop that Nancy is hosting. I still don't feel *any* draw to shave my head—at least not when I enter the room. We begin the group Rebirth and while I'm in the session, Babaji comes to me again and tells me to ask the community who would like to stay for a Mundan Ceremony afterward. I laugh at Babaji during the session and in my inner world I tell myself once again, "Hell no, I'm not doing that!"

After we do a group session, Nancy asks who would like to share their experience. Before I know it my hand is in the air and I'm asking the group to stay for a Mundan Ceremony. I'm thinking to myself, "Whose voice *was* that?!" I don't even know that I've just spoken this out loud.

Soon, I find myself outside at the center of a circle of people singing Indian devotional songs while someone shaves off *all my hair*. While they do this, I watch a silent videotape of my entire life cross over the screen of my mind in fast-forward.

Once shorn, I completely understand why this practice holds such spiritual meaning. With no hair, I feel nothing like the person I had been looking at in the mirror every day for my entire life. *Who am I now?* Certainly not the beautiful woman—at least by Midwestern standards—that I had always aspired to be. I feel naked, vulnerable. And in that nakedness, another kind of beauty has space to emerge, one that wells up from a very deep place within me.

And beyond looks, after they shave off my hair, the crown of my head is now exposed. It feels so sensitive and sensual that I feel more life force. For the first time, I feel a flood of energy come into my head and down into my body. And not only during the ceremony or meditation, but all the time. Who knew?!

At home, the fact that I spend so much time with little Andrew now seems fitting to me. I feel like a baby all over again, being reborn into an unknown world. At work, I begin wearing a wig, which I throw into the back seat of my car as soon as I leave the office. Like a caterpillar's cocoon, the wig helps to cushion me from an unforgiving outside world that would have difficulty understanding why a woman would willingly shave her head. Inside, I feel my old self becoming liquid, mercurial. Who will I be when I emerge from this cocoon? I have no idea.

Since I find myself in a more internal space of transformation, I'm a bit more hesitant with anyone I don't know well, and haven't been adding too many social engagements to the calendar. Nonetheless, I decide to bring some tickets for a popular tennis match over to my friend Martin's house as a surprise—he loves tennis and I had received them as a perk from my job. His home had hosted that memorable birthday party, the one I had attended with Mark just a few days before he died. Even without going back to this house, the night burns fresh in my memory. I replay all its details like a detective looking for evidence—not of a mysterious death, but of my own failure to prevent one.

I give myself a pep talk as I drive over to deliver the tickets. I would make this fast, I tell myself. I would drop off the tickets, then I would head back to Julie and Craig's house, where I could play with baby Andrew.

Instead of my friend Martin, a man named David answers the door after I ring the bell. David had been living there for a while, though I had seen him only once on the night when I last spent time with Mark.

At that party, I had noticed David. I don't think I could have missed him actually, since his charisma had easily filled the room.

He wears a beard and a mustache, and his balding head is encircled with ringlets of curly hair that he pulls back into a low ponytail. When he smiles, his whole face lights up. I learned that he works as a pedorthist—an orthotic and orthopedic footbed specialist—who had built a booming practice in St. Louis that he had later sold. After bouncing around California and Hawaii, he had moved back to spend the year with his son, Jesse, who would soon be a senior in high school. David seems like a rare breed, able to mix responsibility and business know-how with his free-spirited attitude toward life.

But I had only watched David at the party that night from my perch at an open railing on the second floor. Most of the time he spent flirting with another woman. Despite the intimate tone of the gathering, we never actually spoke. Since then, I hadn't given David another thought.

Now we're exchanging pleasantries at the doorstep of that same home in Webster Groves, an upscale suburb of St. Louis. After I hand David the tennis tickets, I continue to talk with him from behind the invisible walls I had erected to deal with Mark's passing.

After a few minutes of chit chat, he senses that I might be concerned about something, and I surprise myself by opening up about Mark. I had isolated myself from talking about it, and I find myself appreciating not feeling alone... having someone deeply listen. This person was meeting me in a place I had never been met by a stranger. Feeling very different now than how I had on the ride over, I get into my car and head home.

When David asks me out a few months later in November, I feel ready to re-enter the world of dating again. At the end of our first date, which happens on his birthday, David hugs me. With this simple gesture, a huge wave of feeling washes over me, so powerful that I have the experience of floating above my body. I know immediately: Whatever this man and I need to experience together would change my life.

David and I are still dating in January 1997 when I receive some rotten news. I have hepatitis C. Researchers had only discovered this strand of hepatitis in 1989. However, I'd likely contracted it way back in 1972 when I was using intravenous drugs.

At least the diagnosis explains why I often feel so exhausted. Still, I feel anything but relieved as I learn about the disease.

After a battery of tests and a biopsy of my liver, I meet with my doctor. To the appointment, I carry the load of guilt and shame I'd been grappling with since the diagnosis. After all, I'd done this to myself! At age 43, I feel as if my life is finally taking off—only to be grounded by a serious illness. The news brings up many of the old thoughts I'd been wrestling with over the years.

My tests, however, show that I'm surprisingly healthy, despite this condition. The doctor starts our meeting by asking what I'd done to keep myself so fit? I explain some of my health regimen, emphasizing the work I'd done with a chiropractor on my liver.

After I finish, the doctor recommends I begin an Interferon regimen, the main drug doctors use to deal with the condition.

I listen politely. When he finishes, I ask, "So doctor, off the record. If your test results had come out as good as mine, what would you do? Would you take this medication?"

"Well, Linda," he said, after a pause and with a little twinkle in his eye, "I do recommend you slow down. A disease like this can really take a toll on your energy levels, and you have a lot of stress in your life. I'll see you in six months."

Apparently, my interest in health and fitness all these years has paid off. Many years before, by following intuitive guidance from Spirit I had even found my way to an innovative chiropractor who specialized in issues with the liver. While he hadn't diagnosed this condition—a task outside the parameters of his practice—his work with me had surely played a major role in keeping me healthy, not to mention all the cleansing, fasting, juicing, exercise, and bodywork I had received along the way. After something like 25 years of unwittingly living with a serious disease, I was faring notably better than most who had gotten diagnosed early and received standard treatment.

Once again, Spirit has cleared the path for me. The effort and energy I had invested in learning how to listen to Spirit and follow the guidance I received are also paying off.

Even so, I leave that appointment in shock. The doctor hadn't really told me point blank that I don't need to take the recommended medication. So should I trust my gut, my guidance, and continue with everything I have been doing so far? Or should I listen to the common protocol and take the meds? If I don't take it, would hep. C kill me? Once again, I need to go deep inside for the answers—*and* find the courage to trust them.

In the end, I decide to stick with natural medicine to treat my condition. I make this choice, not because I don't trust mainstream medical advice, but because my own guidance in this situation tells me to stay the course. My body doesn't want Interferon. I simply know that this medication and I aren't a fit.

With the diagnosis, I feel a new surge of commitment to my health. I read everything I can get my hands on about the liver. I get passionate again about cleansing and fasting and I take extra care with my diet. My reading also reminds me that the liver holds anger, and its neighbor, the gallbladder, resentment. In the spirit of treating my body as best as I can, I begin looking deeply at any old grudges or hurts I still hold.

With new forms of meditation, I learn to quiet my mind and pay attention on a whole new level. The more I practice this seemingly simple feat, the more peaceful I become.

But I still wonder, how will I ever slow down? My job keeps me on the move, and I know it will only get busier as my responsibilities increase. I have no idea how to follow the doctor's orders—his advice for me to slow down. It had made sense when he said it, but I'm now becoming more and more aware of the incredible shifts that taking *this* prescription might require.

"Hummingbird."

David tells me that he and some friends have bought a large piece of land in northern New Mexico where they had been planning to create what he called an "intentional community." Their intentions were to build earthen homes, grow spiritually together, and practice what they were learning. They were calling it Hummingbird.

He had been talking to me about the idea since we started dating, so I had known he would leave St. Louis sooner rather than later, and I had tried to keep him at a distance to avoid the pain of saying goodbye. We could have fun together, yes, but then he would go. Then I would move on to the next person Spirit brings me. That's what I had been telling myself, anyway.

Then in May 1997, David asks me if I will take a leave of absence from work to visit Hummingbird for the summer. Whether I like it or not, I have to admit to myself that I hadn't done a great job of keeping an emotional distance from him. The spark between us makes it tough for me to say no to his request.

On the other hand, I know without even asking that my boss will never let me take a long chunk of leave. I had just gotten a promotion and have a pile of responsibilities in my new position. I'm still learning the job, and there's no one available to take my place for more than a few days at a time.

One evening, not long after David had made his invitation, I have, for lack of a better word, a dream. Actually, it feels more like I'm traveling back to that otherworldly place beyond dreams, the one where I had floated above my body as doctors worked to save my life. Just like before, a visitor comes to me. An angel? A guide? The being and its realm exist in such a different frequency from our physical world and I couldn't so much see, as *sense,* that being's presence— a powerful, loving energy. During this altered dream-state, the visitor tells me very clearly that I need to give a 30-day notice at work, leave the life I've known for the last 30 years, and move to Hummingbird.

I wake in a gasp, like resurfacing from deep waters. The message is still buzzing in my head. Leave everything behind? Why would I do that?! I love my new job. I'd lived in this area for decades, and I have incredible friends, not to mention my home with Julie, Craig, and Andrew. I have a blessed life.

But I cannot deny what I've heard. Even as I immediately start questioning my own sanity, I feel compelled to at least *explore* the idea of moving to Hummingbird.

Over the next two weeks, I begin conversations with my closest friends about the dream and its instructions. To my surprise, every one of them—even Julie and Craig—say they can picture me moving there. I keep thinking: *Really? I can't!* But somehow they all think the notion fits me.

Finally, I go to my father. Because Spirit had led me to live near him until we had healed our painful past together, his opinion now matters the most. I need to ask him what he thinks about my moving to New Mexico.

My mind is debating back and forth the whole ride over. On one hand, I know that Dad is someone who plays it safe, and I would be leaving a good job with a pension, health insurance, and growth opportunities for my career future. He's also unlikely to support the idea of this move since I hadn't really known David for all that long. On the other hand, he does really like him. Another leap of faith... I walk into his house to seek his approval.

"All I want is for you to be happy," he answers to my surprise, and without hesitation.

That settles it. If I have Dad's blessing, then I know I can take this leap with a clear conscience. This also signifies that Dad and I have healed our relationship, and I can take the next step in my life *and* stay connected to him no matter where I am in the world.

After 30 *years*, I now have 30 *days* to transition my life from St. Louis. I'm soon moving to Mora, New Mexico... sight unseen. I'll live in a place called Hummingbird.

As I pack up my life and prepare for the move, I find myself thinking of the way a hummingbird always finds the sweetness of life buried deep within a flower. So small, and yet so powerful, this being that cuts a trail of joy through the summer sky. I love starting my new life on this note.

What will life be like without a nine-to-five job? Waking up and going to sleep with the sun on 486 acres in a lush, green valley surrounded by forest, rivers, and mountains. What will I learn about myself, life, and love? Saying yes to this move feels like a big, looooong exhale. And one that gratefully supports the life journey I've been on. It feels like a natural next step, rather than a leap or more crazy-making.

And I'm not losing my dearest friends and family—I'm taking flight! I'm no longer escaping reality through drugs and alcohol; I'm choosing the grace-filled path. I'm okay diving into the unknown and trusting that life is unfolding as it needs to. After 25 years of recovery, my life is now being shaped by my values, no longer by my traumatic past and the unconsciousness that I had lived in for so many years.

I now know that everywhere I go, there I am.

Lesson & Blessing

#16

All We Are Is Love

At age 17, I attended a party that would change everything. In a normal-looking house, on a normal-looking street, I had wandered past the edges of the normal-looking world of my childhood. In a needle, I had found liquid courage. At age 12, I had found liquid courage in a bottle. Surely, I had stumbled into my own private oasis, an escape from all the pain.

What a mirage it all turned out to be.

More than 25 years later, I had attended another party. Like the first, it took place in suburbia—this time, in an upscale neighborhood with a conscious crowd. Instead of sneaking up the stairs for an illicit drug encounter, I wandered through a Zen interior of shiny, polished wood. I wove in and out of conversations between young professionals and respected community elders, admiring statues of Buddha and Lakshmi along the way. In an inviting sunroom, I peered into a lush backyard. I found no bottles of whiskey or electric wine. In fact, I can't even remember if they served alcohol at all. Folks here passed around musical instruments instead of bottles or pills. We gathered not to shoot up, but to rise up in song.

I had worked hard to get there. This party represented everything I loved about my life. How relaxed I had felt that evening. For the first time, everything in my life seemed handled.

Yet without knowing it, I was standing once again at the threshold between two worlds. A few short days after that party, the best friend on my arm that night would be gone forever.

And a few short months after that, the charismatic stranger across the room would invite me to move halfway across the country, to a culture and lifestyle so different from this one that it might as well have been halfway around the world.

Even more of life's curveballs were continuing to be thrown my way, and of course they still are today. Life is not about having no stress, no challenges, no questioning of what is. When the hepatitis C diagnosis had come, the simultaneous gift of being invited to be part of a soul family at Hummingbird had also arrived. And once again, I learned to quiet my mind and pay attention. I would discover that life's lessons have no end, just ever-deepening levels of understanding and mastery.

And here's what I learned through it all: *I can handle it*. Life can come at me, even topple me over. But I'll get back up again. Instead of running for cover, I'll keep on getting back up. Why not? After all, Spirit has my back. *Always*. I had put this notion to the test over and over again, almost breaking myself in the process. Now, I know it in every bone in my body.

I had spent 25 years of my life learning this lesson. It had taken nothing less than all of me to accomplish the invisible miracle of feeling at home in this world and in my body. I finally had enough presence of mind, body, and heart to catch the curveballs.

I learned a deep love of reaching for the next biggest place inside me, testing my strength against the weight of my life, the way I had tested my body in the gym so many years before. I had surpassed my own mother's hopes for me and found a way to rebuild the love between me and my father. And my mother and I had found a way out of the depths of separation to an intimacy that I have carried forward into all my relations. My relationship with my brother, Ron, went from merely an occasional phone call to one of deep respect, space to share our inner transformations, and shared spiritual journeying that brought additional healing and wholeness to our family. All of this brought a life greater than I had ever thought possible.

Even more than all of this, I had pursued the dream of knowing myself—authentically, from the inside out—with my whole heart. I had chased the questions, "Who am I, and why am I here?" as if my life depended on it. Turns out, it had.

In this chapter, I shared my experiences with a religious tradition from India. Yet, I need to state clearly that you don't need to shave your head, study a new religion, or go to a distant country to take the path of freedom. If something like this calls to you, then follow the voice you hear. But maybe you feel a pull to study art, to learn French cooking, or to travel to Asia. The voice that calls us into our biggest selves has different things to say to each of us. We unlock its messages when we take the time to listen and then take action.

This is the starting place for the guiding principles I learned that would save me from a life of drug and alcohol addiction. These principles would carry me far beyond the realm of recovery, too. They would serve as a road map for my ongoing passage into a bigger, bolder, richer life—the one that I now lead every day. During the journey, I have discovered lasting joy.

Perhaps this is why I eventually became a professional ontological coach. The coaching I received from so many dedicated people revolutionized my life. My many years of being sponsored, then serving as a sponsor and coaching others along the road to freedom, would teach me that the principles of recovery serve as a rock-solid foundation upon which anyone can build a beautiful, powerful life.

The circle of receiving and giving that lies at the center of my own recovery also taught me that none of us achieves miracles alone. Whether or not we're working with addiction, all of us—every last one—is dealing with the same human condition. I love to tell my clients: "With 7.6 billion of us on this planet, do you think any of us is supposed to figure this thing out all by ourselves?!" No one of us is better or worse than another. Just human. And that's enough.

I'm so blessed to be able to say that people who meet me now can't believe the stories about my past as a druggie and a drunk. I've stood before women in homeless shelters, explaining how I didn't graduate from high school, how I lived for several years from needle to needle. To them, it often doesn't seem possible that a person could make such a big turnaround. They tell me how much hope my story brings them.

They have taught me that my many years of addiction and recovery, a fact of my life that once caused me so much shame, have become one of my greatest gifts to the world. By starting in Hell, and eventually making it to a life that often feels to me like Heaven, I serve as a living example. You truly can accomplish anything with the guidance and support of Spirit, which points the way to a supportive community, the realization that you aren't alone, and the healing tools you need to transform your life.

No matter where you are—a small, conservative town, feeling stuck in a loveless marriage, locked in the gruesome cycle of addiction or affected by someone else's addiction, overcome by the pain of loneliness, or just plain living a so-called "normal" life while you yearn for something more—your true essence as love is there. Love exists in these parts of you, too. It has never left you, never will leave you, and it desires only your freedom. It holds all the answers you keep looking for in the world outside, too. It yearns for you to rise up, to go inside. Love itself loves you in the way you've always dreamed someone else would.

Through the writing and editing of this book, I was being shown all along the way that who we really are is Radiant Love, and that our conditioning hides that from ourselves and others. All of our conditioning, anger, resentments, hatred—whatever it is that's unresolved—stands in the way of us being able to receive and feel the radiance of ourselves and others *as* this naturally Loving Presence. We need to go into those hidden places, discover the conditions that keep us continuing to act out a certain habit, feel what we didn't allow ourselves to feel when each behavior began, and free ourselves, one by one.

The *Presence* that invited me back to life that day was actually this Radiant Love—it was me *as* this love, engulfing me in its unconditionality. I didn't need to do, be, say, or think anything in order to be fully accepted. We humans think that we're only our bodies, our minds, our emotions, and our behaviors. But what we *actually* are is, was, and always will be is... LOVE. It's so amazing! We know this when we arrive here as babies, and we can each find our way back to this knowing.

With the recognition that you *are* love, I know—beyond even the smallest crumb of a doubt—that your life, too, is an answered prayer. Right here, right now. In this very breath. You don't have to do anything to earn it either. You simply need to train yourself, if you haven't already, to see the miracle unfolding within you. From here, the seed of your dreams can awaken, grow, and blossom.

Then anything can happen. Truly, anything.

Epilogue

"We delight in the beauty of the butterfly,
but rarely admit the changes it has gone through
to achieve that beauty."
~Maya Angelou

There was this woman named Pam. Now, I don't remember many names, but this woman's name I'll never forget. I had recently moved to the Midwest from southern New Mexico, and she terrorized me. She bullied me. And this went on for quite a while. Finally I got so angry one night I beat the crap out of her in the backyard at a friend's house. She finally hit that place within me. I was under 100 pounds—so she was perhaps twice my size, ginger hair, and a freckled face. And I was so enraged from all of the bullying I'd had throughout my life, so that day I took her down and clobbered the hell out of her. That's the only time in my life I can say I've really gotten into a fight... really beat someone up physically.

But what actually guided me to do this? It wasn't that I didn't like her, or even the anger flowing through me. No, it was the deeply seeded internal message I had thoroughly adopted by then that I was *not* good enough, *not* part of the group, *not* worthy of connection... *not* this, *not* that. And what I realized is that countless experiences in my growing-up years had given these self-perceptions the fertilizer to sprout and grow, and become a stable tree rooted in my psyche and body.

What I know now in all the cells of my body and in the thoughts that emerge moment to moment, is that these self-perceptions were not wrong or false, but they *are* thoroughly outdated. And I didn't need to cut the tree down and grow a new me. Rather, all my life experiences have become like compost. Here at Hummingbird where I still reside, we don't throw much of anything "away." The food scraps, the grass clippings, they all go into a warm, dark, and secure place for a while to be recreated into something new—something useful for the next phase of the garden to grow.

My roots, exactly as they are—Dad, Mom, Ron, drinking and drugging friends, Pam... all of it—have served to support and stabilize part of me so that I could have a foundation upon which to build a new set of perceptions. Without the journey precisely as it is, I would be without the rich soil to evolve into the woman I am today. A woman free from cancer and hepatitis C, living in a rural, intentional community devoted to the evolution of consciousness and growing healthy food; enjoying the richness of loving relationships with people here and around the world, including my brother Ron and his wife, and my father, with whom I have enjoyed bi-annual visits since moving to northern New Mexico.

I now live my life in recognition that each of us is on an evolutionary journey... the road map to life is one that *I* map out. I never needed to be given it in the first place! I live as a whole and complete person and am self-responsible, meaning I'm responsible for my physical, emotional, and spiritual well-being. I live in balance with both the shadow and light in my life and relationships. I know that I'm perfectly imperfect. My belief is that I'm here to learn and to grow as a human being, and that means that I'll inevitably have life experiences that regularly invite me to dig deeper into "soul-utions."

I could describe the universal movement we all experience in life in some form is one from listening to the previous emotions and stories and believing that they're true—believing that we *are* our behaviors—to stepping into what we know is true *now*. And, this isn't the end. There is no end. We're each in an endless evolutionary life with countless lessons and blessings available to be received every step of the way.

P.S. This morning as I sat down to put my final touches on the memoir and send it off to be typeset and then published, I was inspired to add a bit to the Epilogue here to offer you even greater transparency. At this stage in my endless evolution, I'm working on what one might call "stepping up" in life. I've been a Personal Development & Executive Coach for many years, but it's a different story to share so much of one's *life* story with the world. I felt a deep longing when I woke up this morning that said, "I don't want to die knowing I could have helped somebody." I see myself as someone who has something useful to offer to somebody who's looking to move both through and beyond recovery. I'm interested in people who are thinking "There's no f*cking way that I could ever move from where I am to where I dream to be!" That is my biggest care.

Within minutes, I received a text message from someone who wrote: *"Hi Linda—today is my first day choosing to not drink. I am reaching out because I think you said something about recovery when we were talking at that conference last month—and I am dealing with a whole range of emotions—and I guess I am scared. It feels like a bad time to make this choice because I really want to numb out... thank you for reading this."* I immediately realized that now, one of the greatest blessings of my life is precisely this. Receiving you as you are. Being present to the endless evolution of others. Witnessing the exquisiteness of the ever-present composting process in each of us.

So I now let this book fly away... as it is... to be of use in whatever way it can be to whomever finds their way to it. The motivation to share this book and to be of use to others now feels clearly born out of that rich soil that was created through my life's unique experiences. I lived in hell for so long. And when it finally felt like heaven was when I felt true freedom.

To me, Heaven is not that place high in the sky that is described by many religions and professed to be coming one day in the future. It's that place of freedom, of wonderment, where I can more easily receive the gifts of life—both the flow and the challenges. It's meeting life on life's terms. To live in Heaven is to live with emotions like shame, guilt, remorse, and fear, without needing to annihilate them with an addiction. To me, Heaven has to do with being aware of infinite possibility.

Will you join me in creating Heaven together?

Appendix A:
Eyesight During Extreme Drug Use

The National Center for Biotechnology Information states, in an article titled "Ocular Manifestations of Drug and Alcohol Abuse," that "drug and alcohol abuse can produce a variety of ocular and neuro-ophthalmic side effects. Novel, so-called 'designer' drugs of abuse can lead to unusual ocular disorders. Legal substances, when used in manners for which they have not been prescribed, can also have devastating ophthalmic consequences."

I now understand that this is what caused my temporary blindness during my drug usage. And this didn't happen only the one time from the barbiturate overdose shared in Chapter 1. This was a regular occurrence through my addiction years. And once on my recovery journey, I talked about my eyes even changing color. There are many theories about diet affecting eye color, so it's my guess that ridding my body of so many toxins allowed the eyes to find a more natural expression.

Appendix B:
Physiochemical Mechanisms
of Addiction

In recent years, a body of brain research has emerged that explains the physiochemical mechanisms of addiction. Some of the most telling discoveries point to the role of dopamine in a region of the brain called the nucleus accumbens.

The nucleus accumbens is the part of the brain scientists often call the reward center. Here, dopamine tells receptors when you've accomplished important survival-related tasks like eating or sex, to send you a hit of good feelings. In terms of evolution, these things have historically taken lots of hard work to accomplish. Gathering berries, hunting in the woods, or even just winning the affection of a beautiful girl in small tribal gene pools—all required both effort and stamina. By giving us strokes, dopamine ensured we would stay motivated to keep ourselves in the game of survival.

Now consider modern life. Substances like alcohol, heroin, cocaine, and sugar—none of them available to ancient man—offer a host of ways to quickly flood the nucleus accumbens with dopamine.

That's the first hit. The first drink. In the cycle of addiction, nothing will compare to the feeling of the first taste.

Why? This flood of dopamine, which hasn't required any effort to attain, has hit the nucleus accumbens full force. A massive wave of neuro-chemical pleasure lights up the brain and you barely had to lift a finger for it.

Yet these chemicals have hit the brain at a level it doesn't know how to handle. "Hey man," the brain says, "that's some seriously strong stuff. I think we're going to have to make some changes around here if that's the way things are going to be."

So the process of downregulation immediately begins. Down-regulation happens when the brain starts thinning out dopamine receptors in the nucleus accumbens. It's a little bit like drawing the shades in a very sunny room. The next time dopamine floods in, it won't be able to over-flood the nucleus accumbens.

Sounds good, right? The brain is adapting—part of our ability to survive as a species. Unfortunately, though, downregulation means that once a person comes out of a dopamine high, the normal level of dopamine that the brain was working with no longer has a normal number of receptors to hit. Just to feel that level of "normal," you now need more drugs to hit the dopamine that then hits the thinned-out receptors.

In other words, normal doesn't feel normal anymore. Your brain is now functioning with less capacity to feel good, with or without drugs.

With the next hit of heroin—or sugar, pornography, etc.—the brain downregulates a little more. Now high doesn't feel as high as the last time. And once you come down, normal feels even less normal than it did after the first hangover. Eventually you don't even remember what high feels like. The brain has adapted so well that you're hitting the needle, the bottle, the candy machine, or anything that will have you feel better than being in hell.

Appendix C:
Blackout Drinking,
Medically Speaking

I'm passionate about people with addiction receiving the proper diagnosis. It's a disease but is often treated otherwise. As I shared throughout my story, I was often misdiagnosed, by both psychiatrists and my family, as having mental illness or being "crazy," primarily due to blackout drinking.

So, how does blackout drinking affect the brain? It affects both long- and short-term memory, and during blackouts, the memory loss is permanent. You literally have no recollection of where you've been or what you've said. My parents didn't understand this possibility, so the misdiagnosis of mental illness was somewhat understandable! I seemed crazy to them, and I hid my drinking in the beginning, so that contributed to the misdiagnosis as well. I imagine this to be quite common today, and for many people, if they received the proper diagnosis that they have the disease of addiction, now officially named Alcohol Use Disorder (AUD), could be treated properly and have a chance to heal.

Chronology

Because my life stories are shared in this book through the people and incidents, with dates noted only here and there for reference, I decided to include a simple chronology of events in the actual order that they occurred to support you in following the story most easily.

	0	**Birth** Salina, Kansas, December 31,1953
Moved to Japan Japan, 1955	2	
	4	**Grandmother Dies** Topeka, Kansas, 1957
Moved to Illinois Chanute Air Force Base, 1959	5	
	5	**Holdover in Pennsylvania** Uniontown, Pennsylvania, 1959
Moved to Germnay Many locations in Germany, 1959	5	
	9	**Moved to Georgia** Warner Robins Air Force Base, 1963
Expelled from Catholic School Sacred Heart School, 1966	12	
	12	**Moved to New Mexico** Holloman Air Force Base, 1966
Had first drink New Mexico, 1966	12	
	13	**Treated by first psychiatrist** El Paso, Texas, 1967
Moved to Illinois O'Fallon, Illinois, June, 1968	14	
	17	**Entered psych ward** Jewish Hospital, February, 1971
Had abortion Jewish Hospital, March, 1971	17	
	17	**Released from psych ward** O'Fallon, Illinois, June, 1971
Met Hound Dog Swansea, Illinois, June, 1971	17	
	17	**Used first intravenous drug** Belleville, Illinois, July, 1971
Went to Mardi Gras New Orleans, February, 1972	18	

18 **Overdosed**
East St. Louis Hospital, Fall, 1972

Attempted suicide for 2nd time
Scott AFB Hospital, September 11, 1973

19

19 **HELP!**
David P. Wohl in Missouri,
Earned G.E.D. 1973-1974
Belleville, Illinois, May, 1974

20 **Did last hit of heroin**
O'Fallon, Illinois, 1974

20

Went to Belleville College
Belleville, Illinois, Fall, 1974

20

21 **Entered 3rd (final) psych facility**
David P. Wohl in Missouri, 1975

Got job as pharmacy bookkeeper
Edgemont, Illinois, 1977

23

25 **Fred called me a "drunk"**
Double Eagle Saloon, June, 1979

Called A.A. accidentally
Edgemont, Illinois, June, 1979

25

25 **Went to first A.A. meeting**
O'Fallon, Illinois, June, 1979

Made first visit to Hubbard's
Belleville, Illinois, Summer, 1979

25

25 **Completed first day clean & sober**
Belleville, Illinois, August 11, 1979

Began studying Eckankar teachings
Casablanca Hair Salon, 1979

25

26 **Got tattoo**
Belleville, Illinois, 1980

Began powerlifting
Vic Tanny Gym, 1980

26

28 **Got job at alcohol/drug film co.**
Belleville, Illinois, 1982

Married Jeff
Belleville, Illinois, March 13, 1982

28

30 **Began Lakota Path**
Rural Missouri, 1984/85

Job as substance abuse coordinator
Belleville, Illinois, October, 1988

34

35 **Became an insurance agent**
Illinois area, June, 1989

Mom's passing
Belleville, Illinois, March 14, 1989

35

35 **Marked 10th Recovery Anniversary**
Belleville, Illinois, August, 1989

Moved to small apartment
Belleville, Illinois, October, 1989

35

Resources

From my perspective, there's no original thought. Mark Twain believed that every thought and nearly every idea were recycled from other thoughts or ideas, whether it was done on purpose or through some collective unconscious process. I recognize how we can both be original in what we say *and* how we're also interpreting our mentors, teachers, coaches, etc., and our unique life experiences.

In my search for life's deeper meaning, these and many other mentors, authors, and healers inspired me to look more deeply into who I am as soul's embodiment. This list primarily reflects the inspirations during my first 20 years of recovery (the period of life explored in these pages) and includes any I also reference specifically in the book.

I often re-read these books and revisit these teachings, along with so many others not listed here (from the subsequent years not shared in this book). These are presented in no particular order:

<u>Teachings & Mentors</u>
St. Francis of Assisi
Mother Teresa
Eckankar
Haidakhan Babaji
"A Course in Miracles"
Zen Buddhism
Jesus
Sufism

Bahá'í Faith

Edgar Cayce

Sri Ravi Shankar & The Art of Living

Lakota Path

And Oprah, for speaking out despite

being well ahead of her time

Healing Modalities

Arise & Shine® Transformational Cleanse

Herbal Supplements

Juicing/Fasting

Colonics

Bodywork/Rolfing

Chiropractics

Integrative Medicine

Reflexology

Massage Training

Rebirthing & Rebirthing Training

Meditation

Pranic Healing and Reiki Training

Family Constellation

Astrology

Sweat Lodges/Vision Quests

Books & Authors

"The Big Book," by Alcoholics Anonymous

"Twelve Steps and Twelve Traditions," by Alcoholics Anonymous

"As a Man Thinketh," by James Allen

"You Can Heal Your Life," by Louise Kay

"Loving What Is," co-authored by Bryon Katie

"Autobiography of a Yogi," by Paramahansa Yogananda

"The Prophet," by Kahlil Gibran

"The Greatest Miracle in the World," by Og Mandino

"St. George and the Dragon and The Quest for the Holy Grail,"
"The Ethiopian Tattoo Shop" and "Twelve and One-Half Keys,"
by Edward Hays

"The Seat of the Soul," by Gary Zukav

"Women Who Run With the Wolves: Myths and Stories of the
Wild Woman Archetype," by Clarissa Pinkola Estés, Ph.D.

"The Body Keeps the Score," by Bessel van der Kolk

Books by Caroline Myss,

Leo Buscaglia,

Eckhart Tolle,

Richard Moss, MD,

Jack Kornfield,

Wayne Dyer,

Alan Cohen, and

Iyanla Vanzant

And the poetry of Maya Angelou, Hafiz, and Rumi

Acknowledgments

Before I began to write this acknowledgment page I looked up the definition of the word acknowledgment to facilitate the reflection that I needed to begin writing. I discovered that acknowledgment means "an author's statement of indebtedness to others."

I am indebted to so many, beginning with my ancestral lineage. Without the perseverance of my ancestors, I may not have had the strength of character to strive in life. The moment that I began to realize this, a big well of gratitude grew in my heart. It lives with me today.

Thank you to the perfect parents Eleanor Ann Brockman and Robert Arthur Sibert for providing the perfect life situations that had me work hard and dig deep to find meaning and purpose in life. I believe my soul knew exactly what I needed when I chose my parents.

And to my brother Ron who continues to teach me about devotion, loyalty, and how to love and be loved, I have endless gratitude. This book may not have happened without his encouragement, faith, and belief in my story and the gift it might offer to others.

I acknowledge all the seekers who wrote books and shared their curiosities and insights regarding the meaning of life and the evolution of consciousness that have expanded my awareness and wisdom.

Deep gratitude to Dr. Bob and Bill W. for providing a program of recovery that gave me hope that became faith by following the guidelines and working the steps. My heart is full of so many people whom I met in meetings around the world and especially the

O'Fallon Trailer Group in Southern Illinois. The sharing of their experience, strength, and hope laid the foundation for my recovery.

I am also indebted to Marty and Dotty Hubbard who became my surrogate parents once I entered recovery. Through their love and patience I learned commitment, integrity, honor, and devotion. I can't even imagine who I might have become had I not been invited so openly into their home to witness their living example of recovery. Their legacy lives on through their large family and me. They walked beside us until the day of their deaths, and their guidance continues to be felt in my life.

And for the wonderful "cast of characters" I have had the pleasure of knowing who were brought to life within the pages of this memoir. I honor each of you for invoking in me the lessons and blessings that were needed for me to truly become the woman I am today.

And how does one name and acknowledge so many old and new friends who have become family? You know who you are, and I love you "BIG." You have my love, devotion, and loyalty.

When it comes to the encouragement, writing, editing, project management, and design of this book, I am profoundly appreciative to Michelle Williams, Amanda Creighton, Sean Culman, Mark Courtman, Kathy Quinn, David (Dabo) Fischer, Dustin Eli, and Jamie O'Driscoll. For without your dedication and belief in the project it would not have come into fruition.

In 1997, I moved to northern New Mexico to support the creation of an intentional community, Hummingbird. Living in an intimate, land-based community these last 20+ years has allowed me to access peace, wonder, challenge, commitment, and so much more. I learned to turn inward and live from the inside-out. Hummingbird Community is the place I learned to put my life lessons and blessings into embodied, day-to-day practices with each interaction with my neighbors' humanity. While serving as a steward of the land and other living beings who dwell on its nearly 500 acres, I realized that I am part of a much larger whole—a living, growing movement of life. It is at Hummingbird that I learned to live and express my true purpose with its passion and pleasure.

Lastly, I often say that the third most important thing I ever did in my life (after A.A. and Hummingbird) was attend Newfield Network Ontological Coaching Training. There I learned how to put everything together that I had learned up until that point. It allowed me the opportunity to know how to access my "nature of being" (this is what ontology means) in all my relationships. A special thanks to Julio Olalla, Founder; Veronica Olalla-Love, Global CEO; Deanne Prymek; and Debby Weber for encouraging my journey. Newfield Network's models and distinctions supported me to tap into my essential expression, which I am now able to share out into the world.

I stand on the shoulders of giants.

About the Author

A typical, disoriented military child who moved from place to place, Linda couldn't find her sense of belonging in school, with friends, and even in her own family. Life became unbearable from a very young age. So, she found her way to alcoholism and then drug addiction to soothe the suffering, among countless other horrific strategies. This early loss of her innocence created an insatiable search for the meaning of her existence, questioning: *Why am I here, and what is it all about?*

Through the extraordinary journey of recovery, she slowly but surely came to trust her own body, emotions, and mind, as well as that of others who seemed to genuinely care. Upon this foundation, she began to understand what gifts life could offer. She has explored her ancestral lineage, the many facets of addiction, countless healing modalities, and the both terrifying and intimate experience of making amends one by one. Now, she sees and experiences the blessing in addiction... that hell and heaven are actually one energy, and she uses these self- and life-realizations to support people worldwide in uncovering their inner brilliance.

She found her way, not *out* of addiction, but *through* it, by healing herself and each of her relationships, and has now created an amazing life on a 486-acre "Garden of Eden" intentional community that she co-founded in the mountains of New Mexico. She has both reclaimed the intimacy with her family of origin as well as discovered a family of friends all over the world.

Linda has found passion, purpose, and pleasure in both her personal and professional life. As an Ontological Coach, Author, and Educator, she has combined an intense love of learning with a passion for uncovering the deepest, most authentic drivers of human motivation for sustainable change.

Linda is now often referred to as "Shekinah." Although she responds to her given name, Shekinah is actually her preferred name, and means "divine feminine light of God." While she had never wanted or needed to change her name, when the invitation arose to take on this additional title, she came to understand it as both a name to grow into and as a way to teach her to embrace us *all* as this light. The name her mother and father gave her—Linda—means "most beautiful," so her full name now is *the most beautiful divine feminine light of God*, and that's something we're all becoming.

Lightning Source UK Ltd.
Milton Keynes UK
UKHW010817070921
390173UK00003B/420